The Sacrifice of Jesus

D1447341

FACETS

Selected Titles in the Facets Series

The Sacrifice of Jesus
Understanding Atonement Biblically

Christian A. Eberhart

Fortress Press
Minneapolis

THE SACRIFICE OF JESUS
Understanding Atonement Biblically

Cover image: © istockphoto.com/Andesign101
Cover design: Ivy Palmer Skrade

Library of Congress Cataloging-in-Publication Data
Eberhart, Christian.
  The sacrifice of Jesus : understanding atonement biblically / Christian A. Eberhart.
    p. cm.
  Includes bibliographical references and index.
  ISBN 978-0-8006-9738-9 (alk. paper)
  1. Sacrifice—Biblical teaching. 2. Atonement—Biblical teaching. 3. Violence—Religious aspects—Christianity. 4. Jesus Christ—Crucifixion. I. Title.
  BS680.S2E24 2011
  232'.4—dc22

                                        2011004850

The paper used in this publication meets the minimum requirements of American National Standard for Information Sciences — Permanence of Paper for Printed Library Materials, ANSI Z329.48-1984.

Manufactured in the U.S.A.

15   14   13   12   11   1   2   3   4   5   6   7   8   9   10

For Ted and Betty Warren
I cherish your support, friendship,
and love in my heart.

Contents

Illustrations

Map of ancient Israel and Judah, p. 33.

Fig. 1 (p. 36). Ground Plan of the Tabernacle according to Milgrom, 2004, p. 19.

Fig. 2 (p. 37). Ark of the Covenant, drawing by Yanis Emmanuel Eberhart.

Fig. 3 (p. 48). Altar of Burnt Offering at the Temple of Jerusalem, drawing by Yanis Emmanuel Eberhart.

Map of Jerusalem in Jesus' time, p. 51.

Preface

The present book deals with a difficult topic. Neither the notion of sacrifice nor that of atonement is popular today. And yet these topics are central to Christianity: notions of sacrifice and atonement articulate nothing less than human salvation. Over the past years this dilemma has motivated me to dedicate much time and work to this subject. I am gratified with the generous reception accorded to the work that I produced during this time, specifically to my book *Studien zur Bedeutung der Opfer im Alten Testament: Die Signifikanz von Blut- und Verbrennungs-riten im kultischen Rahmen* (English: "Studies on the Meaning of Sacrifices in the Old Testament: The Significance of Blood and Burning Rites in a Cultic Setting"). It is my hope that the present publication, with its wider scope, will be received with equal interest and may stimulate many more discussions.

I would like to thank those students who attended my course dedicated to this topic. Discussing this subject matter with them convinced me time and again that sacrifice and atonement are relevant today and worth studying. I owe much to their critical feedback. I would also like to express my gratitude to my colleagues in the Sacrifice, Cult, and Atonement Group of the Annual Meeting of the Society of Biblical Literature who have pursued this theme with scholarly rigor and affection over the past years. Rhetta, Steve, Bill, and Jason, you have taught me a lot. It was at one such Annual Meeting that I was first approached by members of the Fortress Press team who invited me to present my new ideas on sacrifice in a concise format. I wish to express my cordial gratefulness to Neil Elliott, Scott Tunseth, Andy Seal, Jackie Nunns, and everyone else at Fortress for their initiative, patience, and continued interest in my work.

Je voudrais spécialement remercier ma femme Véronique qui s'est beaucoup intéressée au sujet de ce livre. I am deeply thankful to her and also to my sons, Yanis and Yonas, for their love and support while I was writing this book and beyond this time.

Introduction
Modern Christianity and the "Sacrifice of Jesus"

When we think about the customary symbols that are in use today to represent the major world religions, such as the six-pointed Star of David representing Judaism, or the crescent moon and star representing Islam, a cross typically comes to represent Christianity. This is no surprise. The cross is a characteristic feature at the top of steeples of modern church buildings of all Christian denominations, including Greek and Russian Orthodoxy. Crosses are, furthermore, located within the actual worship space of many churches; small and large crosses adorn the pulpit or the altar or are positioned at one end of the sanctuary space. The crucifix, a cross featuring a representation of the tortured body of Jesus, is especially popular in the Roman Catholic tradition. (Etymologically, the term *crucifix* is derived from the Latin words *cruci fixus* and means "[one] fixed to the cross.") During worship services in some traditions, Christian ministers repeatedly make the sign of the cross, and this is usually repeated by the assembly of worshipers. This practice is very ancient: already in 204 C.E., the church father Tertullian (ca. 160–ca. 220 c.e.) wrote that Christians had the practice of tracing the sign of the cross on their foreheads.[1]

The cross has come to represent Christianity because the Gospel stories recount that Jesus of Nazareth was crucified by the Romans. The New Testament contains four Gospels that narrate the story of Jesus. At times these Gospels differ considerably in how they recount this story.[2] Yet they all agree that Jesus died on a cross. Indeed, the four passion stories that convey in detail how Jesus was betrayed, arrested, sentenced to death, tortured, executed, and buried (Mark 14–15; Matt 26–27; Luke 22–23; John 18–19) feature the highest degree of similarity of all the various elements of the Gospels. Thus the passion story can be considered as the most stable element of the entire gospel tradition.

What does the cross represent? Without a doubt, still today it conveys that Jesus died a cruel and tragic death. Christians believe and proclaim, however, that the death of Jesus on the cross was more than just a tragedy or an accident. As soon as the message of the resurrection began to spread, the cross was understood as a key symbol of salvation. The apostle Paul wrote already in 54–56 c.e.: "For the word about the cross is foolishness to those who are perishing, but to us who are being saved it is the power of God" (1 Cor 1:18). When asked what the cross represents, many Christians today still affirm a statement like this. And, more than that, since its earliest beginnings, the Christian church has celebrated the salvation on the cross at Easter.

But *how* does the cross save? Or, to ask more precisely: How can people imagine that the death of Jesus on the cross could have saved humanity? In responding to this important question, the Christian church has often referenced the idea of the *sacrifice* of Jesus. The Roman Catholic Church, for example, considers the celebration of the Eucharist as a sacramental reenactment of the sacrifice of Jesus on the cross. This is conveyed, on the one hand, by the fact that Roman Catholic churches feature *altars* on which bread and wine, the two elements of the Eucharist, are prepared by *priests*. Is not an altar the location of sacrifice? And was it not the task of priests in Judaism as well as in other religions to perform sacrifices at sacred locations?

For many Protestants, on the other hand, the statement that "Jesus Christ died for us" captures their core conviction of what Christianity is all about. Sure enough, the New Testament Gospels present the life, passion, death, and resurrection of Jesus of Nazareth as one continuous narrative. Yet S. Mark Heim observes: "Saved by blood, Christians are charter bound to glorify sacrifice."[3] The much-disputed 2004 movie *The Passion of the Christ* reduced the life and resurrection to marginal flash scenes while focusing on Christ's passion and death. Due to its graphic violence, the movie was rated "R" by the Motion Picture Association of America; nevertheless, as many as 31 percent of all U.S. Americans watched it within barely two months of its release.[4] Confronted with its perceived anti-Jewish tendencies, Mel Gibson, who had coproduced, cowritten, and directed the movie, insisted: "The film was less about who killed Jesus and more about his willing sacrifice on behalf of mankind."[5] Many considered the movie to convey what Christianity is all about.

These two examples may suffice to illustrate that today the term *sacrifice* is often employed in order to articulate how the death of Jesus on the cross saves humanity. The "sacrifice of Jesus," then, is a concept that is central to theological reflection and church proclamation of all Christian denominations. In this book I provide a detailed study of the meaning of sacrifice by investigating its roots in the Hebrew Bible and Judean literature and its understanding in the New Testament.

In the Christian Church and theology, any discussion of the death of Jesus, of the cross, of salvation, or of sacrifice falls under the category of atonement. This term was coined in 1526 by William Tyndale to literally mean "at-one-ment." It presupposes that humans and God are separate; humans cannot simply communicate or interact with God. Religious concepts that envision how this separation can be overcome belong to the category of atonement. Furthermore, atonement usually conveys the idea that humans are in a state of bondage to sin. Atonement thus describes some kind of liberation of humans from sin and how they can enter into a renewed relationship with God.[6] A study of the concept of the sacrifice of Jesus by necessity touches upon atonement.

Yet while sacrifice and atonement are core concepts to theological reflection and church proclamation, they both share the same problem: people in our modern—or rather, postmodern—Western world find them difficult to accept. Recognizing this fact, Stephen Finlan wrote a book titled *Problems with Atonement,* in which he comments as follows on the literature of the last 150 years dealing with this topic: "The agenda is largely set by the widespread dismay regarding the received doctrines of atonement."[7] Finlan's statement can just as well be extended to modern perceptions of the concept of sacrifice or the sacrifice of Jesus. It is no less encountered with dismay today.[8]

Objections to Sacrifice

What are the reasons for this negative response to core Christian concepts? Out of many objections, I want to mention four.[9]

First, sacrifice and atonement are perceived as being necessarily connected to death. Some today think that the very center of Israelite/Judean worship was occupied by an institution bent on the ritual annihilation of life, suggesting that Levitical priests should be considered "butchers." Similar views apply to modern perceptions of atonement. For instance, in August 2008, when I interviewed people regarding this topic, one person responded: "I feel that the traditional doctrine of atoning death is nothing but repulsive; for me it is connected to a sadistic image of God. For a long time, the doctrine of atoning death prevented me from having a liberating faith."[10] It is typical that, while the question I had asked was about *atonement*, this person's reply focused on *atoning death*. In Christianity, the phrase that Christ came to "die for our sin" is referenced so often that death has come to be considered as a *conditio sine qua non*, which means that death appears to be the necessary prerequisite for salvation: without death, there seems to be no salvation. This concern applies just as well to New Testament passages about the "blood [of Jesus]" (Heb 12:24; see also 1 Pet 1:2). Yet if atonement is necessarily connected to Christ's blood and death, then we need to ask ourselves the question: Why do Christians not value Christ's life, particularly when it comes to the issue of salvation?

The second reason for negative responses to the topics of sacrifice and atonement is a consequence of this first one. It is rather clear that these two concepts trouble many because they appear to be inherently violent. If blood and death are at the heart of Christianity, does this not amount to a glorification of bloodshed and murder? And would such sacred violence not determine Christian morals and ethics? If the cruel death of Jesus is regularly commemorated during the Last Supper/ Eucharist, why would Christians avoid violence? Given the reality of our war-torn world, this concern leads to a further question: How do Christians come to value peace?

A third concern arises from the Christian belief that Jesus is the Son of God, the divine Father. If this Father is seen as sending his Son on a mission to die, or if this Father is seen as demanding that an innocent person die for others who are guilty, does this not lead to a portrayal of God as a divine child abuser? How could a God of love be recognized behind such immoral scenarios? This concern leads to the question: What is the basis of Christian morals if God is understood either to require that humans offer a bloody sacrifice in order to achieve divine appeasement, or, alternatively, to need the sacrifice of his own Son in order to grant forgiveness?

Fourth, Christians believe that Jesus died for humans. This is the core of the idea of vicarious salvation or substitution: someone who is innocent suffers and dies for someone else who is guilty. In our postmodern world, which heralds individualism and has lost any sense of corporate self-definition, this concept of vicarious salvation has become hard to comprehend. Are we not ultimately responsible for our own sins? Further, if Christians confess in the Apostles' Creed that "Christ will come again *to judge the living and the dead,*" where does the value of his death as substitution fit in?

Such profound concerns and questions are disconcerting specifically when we acknowledge that they are not about some marginal or irrelevant aspect of Christianity. They have to do with the question of how salvation is imagined and communicated. They are, therefore, about core issues of Christianity and are relevant to all Christians. Ultimately, these concerns pose a fundamental question as to how Christians understand grace. Thus Harold Wells asks: "If we preach the grace of God, and derive our personal and social ethic from it, are we thereby implicated in a 'retributive' doctrine about a God who insists on being paid in blood as the price of grace? Does grace, then, cease to be grace?"[11] We see that these questions affect many core elements of Christianity.

Since atonement determines to a large degree how Christians in church, society, and academy construe their identities, it is probably justified to say that we are dealing with issues that represent a Christian identity crisis.

What solutions can we propose to these concerns? Would Christianity not be better advised to abandon problematic concepts such as sacrifice or atonement, and with them to avoid the Scripture passages from which they are derived?[12] Christianity cannot, however, dispose of Jesus Christ and the story about him; if it did, it would cease to be Christianity. And because of the particular person and story of Jesus Christ, Christianity needs to deal with the cross. Despite all of the previously mentioned problems and concerns, sacrifice and atonement are necessary concepts for the explanation of how Jesus saved the world, and how this salvation was effectively achieved without human contribution. Most attempts to avoid these concepts ultimately also avoid talking about a critical and unique part of the story of Jesus, or they fail to convey how salvation has been achieved for humans. This means that many alternatives to sacrifice and atonement, or the avoidance of these concepts altogether, have a tendency to replace the salvation achieved by Jesus with some form of human activity. They have a tendency to promote, more or less openly, human self-salvation.

In addition, atonement is a nonnegotiable component of Christianity, as it constitutes the frame of reference of the Eucharist, or Last Supper. This celebration cannot be understood fully without an attempt at explaining atonement images. In the devotional practice of most Christian denominations, the Eucharist/Last Supper appears to be the climax of worship. As we will see later, it combines references to the story of Jesus Christ, the cross, and atonement. Due to this, many who object to the concepts of sacrifice and atonement usually implicitly or explicitly object to the eucharistic celebration or its message as well. The Eucharist/Last Supper, however, not only conveys salvation in a liturgical form. It also invites people into experiencing salvation and, in doing so, uses atonement images and language. Whoever abandons atonement, therefore, also abandons necessary modern efforts of understanding the roots and essence of this climactic celebration of Christianity.

As we devote ourselves, then, to the study of these much-disputed concepts of sacrifice and atonement, it turns out that few people today are really familiar with them, and even fewer would claim that they deeply understand their meaning or can clearly explain what they are all about. Similarly, few people today would claim to be familiar with the Bible passages from both the Hebrew Bible and the New Testament on which these concepts are based. For example, the concepts of sacrifice and atonement that early Christians used to articulate the meaning of salvation in Christ are primarily metaphors. They are largely derived from the Hebrew Bible and more specifically from the book of Leviticus. The Hebrew Bible belongs to the canon of sacred Scriptures of both Judaism and Christianity. Yet for Christians, various books of the Hebrew Bible remain more or less unknown. And while Leviticus is one of the most cherished writings among many Jews, it tends to be one of the most neglected and least familiar biblical books for Christians.[13] Likewise, it appears that Christianity has, since its earliest days, fostered reservation regarding rituals. Still today, this attitude negatively affects the perception of sacrificial rituals.[14] Thus, familiarizing ourselves with concepts such as sacrifice and atonement requires, first, that we remain open to encountering texts in some of these neglected books of the Hebrew Bible. As we explore these passages and related concepts, many of the concerns mentioned previously will appear in a decisively different light. This means that several concerns regarding sacrifice and atonement are primarily the result of a lack of biblical knowledge and ensuing misconceptions.[15]

Any study of biblical texts, however, requires, second, that the reader be open to explore the realities of the past cultures from which these texts emerged. Toward that end, I occasionally provide additional information and archaeological data. Some of the misconceptions about sacrifice and atonement are, third, the consequence of a lack of comprehension of ancient Judaism. The topic of this book reveals a deep connection, rather than discontinuity, between the Judean/Jewish and Christian traditions, however. Hence, understanding key aspects of Christian soteriology requires at least some familiarity with ancient Israelite and Judean practices and traditions. This study is a conscious attempt of engaging long-standing traditions that are still prominent among Jews today.

On the pages that follow, I present a new vision of core texts of the Hebrew Bible on sacrifice. I argue that the meaning of sacrificial rituals that formed the heart of ancient Israelite and Judean worship—and that still serve as a key referent in rabbinic Judaism—is to be construed as *approach*, *exchange*, *communication*, and *purification*. These rituals lack any particular emphasis on death or violence. This vision has ramifications for how Christians understand the sacrifice of Jesus. I will show how sacrificial motifs have been appropriated in the New Testament and reexamine their christological implications. In particular, I will show that New Testament soteriology does not focus exclusively on the death of Jesus but has a *broader incarnational dimension that includes his entire mission and life.*

This book thus deals with sacrifice as it appears in the Hebrew Bible primarily in the form of rituals and in the New Testament primarily in the form of metaphors. Atonement will be discussed to the degree that it is the "effect" of such sacrifices and belongs to the language of sacrificial metaphors.[16]

All translations of biblical passages, unless otherwise indicated, are my own. I include a glossary of terms, featuring Hebrew and Greek terms, at the end of the book.

1

Rereading the Hebrew Bible
Discovering the Sacrificial Cult

And Noah . . . sacrificed burnt offerings on the altar.
When YHWH smelled the pleasing odor,
YHWH said in his heart, "I will never again
curse the ground because of humankind."
GENESIS 8:20-21

And Moses took the blood [of the sacrifices]
and sprinkled it on the people. And he said,
"See the blood of the covenant that YHWH
has made with you in accordance with all these words."
EXODUS 24:8

What do people in the modern Western world mean when they talk about "sacrifice"?

This term is usually understood to convey that somebody suffers loss for a particular cause or for the sake of a greater good.[17] It is particularly associated with misfortune or the violent destruction of something, for example, the material being sacrificed or a human life. Such a contemporary understanding is evident, for instance, in a song by Billy Joel that describes a war orphan as a "child of sacrifice," or another song by Mika that describes life as involving both love and sacrifice— "a little bit of heaven, but a little bit of hell." Such a negative understanding of sacrifice corresponds to many theories of sacrifice in both theological and anthropological scholarship. In what follows, I shall provide a chronological outline of several theories of sacrifice that have been most influential in these disciplines.[18]

Scholarly Theories of Sacrifice

Bähr and Vicarious Contact with God

Attempts to understand sacrificial rituals are by no means modern endeavors. Already in 1837 and 1839, the German pastor Carl Christian Wilhelm Felix Bähr published a comprehensive study in two volumes titled "Symbolism of the Mosaic Cult."[19] Its section on sacrificial rituals features a distinctive theory of sacrifice based on the idea of substitution. It presupposes that the earthly realm is separated from the heavenly due to human sin. Bähr's core question then is: How can humans ever establish contact with God if either one belongs to a different world? For Bähr, sacrifice is a means of connecting these worlds, and this happens, more specifically, through sacrificial blood rites. He states that "bloody sacrifices" are more important than nonbloody ones since they convey more fully what sacrifice is all about.[20] Instrumental for understanding such bloody sacrifices is Leviticus 17:11: "For the life of the flesh is in the blood, and

I have given it to you to make atonement for your-
selves on the altar, because the blood makes atonement through the life." Bähr takes this passage to
refer to the sinful human life that he understands
to have been transferred to the sacrificial animal.
Since the blood of the animal is applied to parts
of the sanctuary, Bähr reasons that ultimately the
human life is being brought into contact with the
place of the divine presence; this is how substitution occurs.[21] The blood of the sacrificial animal is, therefore, a means through which humans,
despite being fundamentally separate from God,
can establish contact with God.

Sacrifice as Communal Totemistic Meals

Later in the nineteenth century, two Scottish
scholars based their theories of sacrifice particularly on their attention to meals. In 1889, William Robertson Smith, orientalist and professor
of Old Testament, published comparative studies
titled *Lectures on the Religion of the Semites.*[22] Six
of its eleven lectures are dedicated to sacrifice,
which he associates with concepts of taboo and
communion. According to Smith, animal sacrifices
in the Semitic world were generally the settings
for communal meals. Such joyful events constituted and affirmed not only the unity of the clan
or tribe members but also the unity of humans
with the deities who were usually perceived to be
their ancestors. Both levels of communion were
understood to sustain the life of the community.
Yet sacrifice changed with cultural developments:
"When men cease to eat raw or living flesh, the

blood, to the exclusion of the solid parts of the body, comes to be regarded as the vehicle of life and the true *res sacramenti*."[23]

Smith's approach and findings influenced scholars in a variety of fields, among them the cultural anthropologist Émile Durkheim; the founder of psychoanalysis, Sigmund Freud; and the Scottish social anthropologist James George Frazer. The latter coupled sacrifice with totemism in his voluminous study *The Golden Bough* (first published in 1890 and gradually expanded to twelve volumes between 1906 and 1915).[24] According to Frazer, members of primitive clans or tribes understood each other to be connected through kinship ties that originate in totems, that is, common human or nonhuman ancestors. These totems later evolved into deities. Since communal meals were the setting of sustaining life and reinforcing communal ties, Frazer assumes that these meals were ultimately about eating the totemistic deity.

Hubert/Mauss and the Idea of Consecration through Identification

From the end of the nineteenth century dates a lengthy essay titled "Sacrifice: Its Nature and Function," which soon attained the status of a classic and determined the general interpretation of sacrificial rituals for many decades.[25] It was cowritten by the French sociologists and anthropologists Henri Hubert and Marcel Mauss, who both worked at the *École Pratique des Hautes Études* in Paris. Their essay on sacrifice tackles the main question:

How is consecration achieved during the process of sacrifice?

In order to define the essence and function of the "drama" of sacrifice, Hubert and Mauss present a comparative study of sacrificial rituals in Hinduism and in the Hebrew Bible, enriched by occasional examples of Greco-Roman and other cults. Refusing attempts of reducing sacrifice to any single idea, they maintain the complexity of its forms and appearances. Nevertheless, Hubert and Mauss soon focus their study on animal sacrifice.[26] They understand a sacrifice as a consecration of both the victim and the layperson offering it; either one is transformed through a movement from the profane to the sacred realm.[27] The consecration of the victim, on the one hand, occurs in the act of slaughter, which "liberates" the spirit of the sacrificial animal from its physical body. Slaughter is therefore considered the culmination of sacrifice.[28] The consecration of the layperson, on the other hand, is marked by two ritual elements that ultimately constitute a transfer of identity: First, the layperson establishes direct physical contact with the sacrificial animal through the hand-leaning rite or an equivalent action; from now on, she or he is represented through the victim.[29] Second, the layperson partakes of the sacredness "accumulated" in the victim by eating portions of it.[30] Through the interpretation of sacrificial rituals in relation to myths, Hubert and Mauss take their conclusions even one step further: In the end, they conclude that the victim itself becomes divine; animal sacrifice is, in its essence, a sacrifice of the deity.[31]

Koch and Rendtorff: Renewed Interest in Sacrifice and Focus on the Sin Offering

A few other theories of sacrifice have been formulated early in the twentieth century, but overall the interest in matters of the sacrificial cult declined. Reversing this trend, the German Old Testament scholars Klaus Koch and Rolf Rendtorff established a tradition of renewed interest in this subject toward the middle of the twentieth century. According to Koch, the sin offering is a ritual of transferring human sin to a sacrificial animal; sin is then eliminated through slaughter of the animal.[32] Rendtorff questioned this hypothesis. He contributed the specific idea that atonement effects the elimination of both human sin and impurity and contributed a comprehensive study on the development of sacrificial rituals in the Old Testament.[33]

Burkert and the Hunt as the Origin of Sacrifice

The year 1972 saw the release of two very influential studies on the topic of sacrifice: Walter Burkert published a book with the Latin title *Homo Necans*, meaning "The Killing Human,"[34] while René Girard published *Violence and the Sacred*.[35] The titles of both studies set the agenda for the respective analyses of the origins and interpretation of sacrifice. Furthermore, the approaches of both scholars are similar in that both explain sacrifice mostly through their interpretation of ancient Greek myths. To begin with, Burkert, a German classical philologist, wonders: Can "biological" origins of sacrifice be determined? And what is the connection between violence and religion or, by extension, between violence and human society?

Burkert assumes that sacrifice originated in Paleolithic hunting practices. A hunt did not only provide food. It also had, first, a consolidating effect on human clans and tribes as they needed to settle inner disputes in order to join their forces and become a successful hunting party. Second, the hunt also allowed aggressions within the community to be redirected at the animal prey. The success of the hunt is manifest in its decisive moment, the kill. According to Burkert, the primitive human community was unconsciously aware of the positive group-dynamic and life-sustaining effects of the hunt. Therefore, mythic traditions were developed so as to commemorate, and reflect upon, this crucial endeavor, and sacrifice was instituted to ritualize killing.[36] Myths and sacrificial rituals as vehicles of religion made the positive effects of hunting continuously available at the heart of human society. Yet they also depict the human as dependent on killing for the sake of survival, thus revealing the *homo necans*. Burkert finally postulates that killing constitutes the core of religion.[37] Christianity, in his opinion, is no exception in this regard.[38]

Girard and Sacrifice as Generative Sacred Violence

René Girard is a French literary critic, historian, and social anthropologist. Most of his work is dedicated to the following questions: Do ancient Greek drama and literary classics of the Western tradition, albeit fictitious, convey some kind of truth about the existential situation of humanity? And, like Burkert, he asks: Do they offer an explanation for the connection between violence and religion? Based on his analysis of classical literature and anthropological data, Girard develops a comprehensive theory of human society. This literature, while indeed mostly fictitious, reveals human social behavior as being governed by a tendency to imitate others out of rivalry, envy, and jealousy. Girard calls this tendency "mimetic desire." Such behavior leads to ever-escalating conflicts within society, establishing vicious circles of "reciprocal violence."[39] In their efforts to cope with these problems, humans tend to choose outsiders of society, for example members of different ethnic groups or people with injuries, as victims or scapegoats. Cultural order is, according to Girard, typically a response to a crisis.[40] After projecting its problems onto these scapegoats, the dominant society eventually kills them. Girard thus offers an explanation for the disturbing phenomenon that, throughout human history, ethnic and religious minorities (for instance, Jews) were periodically discriminated against and persecuted. He calls this type of corporate mob aggression "generative violence"[41] since it "generates," at least for a moment, relief in the face of an endless spiral of reciprocal violence.

This experience of relief lies at the basis of religion and is, therefore, considered sacred. Humanity reenacts this experience in sacrificial rituals by substituting an animal for the human scapegoat. Thus Girard, like Burkert, defines sacrifice as an act of killing, specifically as collective murder.

An essential feature of the scapegoat mechanism is that those perpetuating it remain unconscious of these "things hidden since the foundation of the world."[42] However, Girard claims that this mechanism is exposed in several biblical stories, for instance those of Abel and Joseph, because they maintain the innocence of the victims. The mechanism is ultimately revealed, and thus forever broken, in the New Testament Gospel narratives since they depict Jesus as being subjected to corporate mob violence but reject the illusion that such aggression could rightfully be directed toward him. Portrayed as the blameless Lamb and the innocent servant of God, Jesus is indeed a scapegoat of society. Thus the hidden mechanism of generative violence is exposed. All humans who become aware of this mechanism are invited to renounce it and instead to engage in peaceful behavior. In light of this, Girard is critical of christological approaches or atonement theologies that depict Jesus once more as a sacrifice.[43]

Gese and Atonement as Substitutionary Incorporation into the Holy

The quest for the meaning of sacrifice continued in the field of religious studies as well. In 1977, Hartmut Gese, professor of Old Testament at the University of Tübingen in Germany, published the essay "The Atonement,"[44] in which he describes sacrifice as a vicarious process. Gese's key question is: How could ancient Israelites and Judeans and, on the other hand, early Christians communicate with the holy God given the general human stigma of sin?

For Gese, "sinfulness . . . is irreparable. It involves guilt that encompasses life itself, a situation where one's existence is forfeit."[45] Given this human predicament, it is God who provides atonement (Hebrew root *kpr*) to reestablish contact with humans. Sacrifices are a ritualized way of achieving such atonement. Several assumptions pave the way for Gese's theory: First, while biblical texts distinguish between different types of sacrifice, Gese presupposes that "those which involve the shedding of blood occupy a special place."[46] Second, he thinks that, in postexilic times, the entire sacrificial cult served the purpose of atonement. And third, he goes on to claim that the sin offering (*ḥaṭṭā't*) became the main paradigm of all types of animal sacrifice.

For Gese, atonement is essentially accomplished through two essential features: the hand-leaning gesture[47] and the blood rite. When the offerer places one hand on the animal's head, Gese affirms that she or he identifies with the sacrificial animal and thus transfers his or her identity. The process of atonement concludes through the blood ritual. After the sacrificial animal is slaughtered, its blood is sprinkled within the space of Israel's sanctuary. It is particularly brought into contact with the Ark of the Covenant, the very place of God's presence. This act is to be interpreted in light of the previous act of identification with the animal: "By a substitutionary sacrifice of life, Israel is brought into contact with God himself. In a ceremony that enacts the approach to God's presence even to the point of ultimate physical contact and still preserves the outward sublimity of that contact in the sprinkling of the drops of blood, the primeval phenomenon of the saving encounter with God is carried out."[48] This atonement cult, provisional in nature, later provides the paradigm for the early Christian understanding of atonement through the death of Jesus.[49] With these features, Gese's understanding of atonement is reminiscent of earlier theories of sacrifice, particularly those of Bähr and Hubert/Mauss. It became very influential, especially in German theology.

Milgrom and Sacrifice in Jewish Interpretation

The Jewish rabbi Jacob Milgrom was professor of Hebrew Bible at the University of California, Berkeley. Facing a tradition of interpretive approaches to cult and sacrifice dominated by Christians, his core question is: What does the Jewish tradition contribute to this debate? In his earlier works, Milgrom applied insights from this rich tradition especially to the interpretation of the sin offering; later he broadly drew on it for the writing of voluminous commentaries on the books of Leviticus and Numbers.

Milgrom begins his new interpretation of the sin offering with a fundamental insight about sin. As a burden for human individuals, sin is forgiven through remorse. Yet depending on its severity, sin also has the effect of staining Israel's sanctuary.[50] Rabbinic interpretation of Scripture emphasizes that the specific purpose of the sin offering is not the elimination of human sin but of the defilement of Israel's sanctuary. Hence, Milgrom prefers to call the sin offering a "purification offering."[51] Such purification is achieved through sacrificial blood: While the priest applies it in special areas or to various objects of the sanctuary, the defilement is transferred to the body of the sacrificial animal. It is finally eliminated when the animal is either burned outside the sanctuary or eaten by the priests.[52]

Sacrifice from the Perspective of Ritual Studies

During the past centuries, a multitude of scholarly theories of sacrifice has been proposed. They have centered on ever new aspects or have interpreted sacrifice from ever new perspectives. Critical of the arbitrariness of these choices, some scholars have recently questioned the basic tenet that sacrifices must be seen as symbols that represent something else, for example, food, and that sacrifice can only be understood from within a larger interpretive framework. These scholars are also critical of previous tendencies to single out particular sacrificial procedures while neglecting others. They ask: Is not each distinct ritual procedure, or each sacrificial ritual as a whole, inherently multivalent? Is a ritual not meaningful through the entirety of its actions? And can sacrificial rituals not convey meaning immediately, that is to say, through their actual gestures? Such questions can lead to a critical attitude toward any interpretive framework and thus also toward religious systems as such. In the words of Ithamar Gruenwald: "In my understanding of rituals and their ritual theory, there is no room for the inevitable inclusion of theological considerations."[53] These larger interpretive frameworks are frequently referred to as "ideologies." Representatives of this approach turn to anthropology, ritual studies, and other disciplines to guide their readings of sacrificial rituals. For example, William K. Gilders, professor of Hebrew Bible at Emory University, argues that sacrificial blood rites in the Hebrew Bible create direct connections or establish immediate meaning.[54] They indicate the privileged social status of priests who are in charge of rituals and mark the sanctuary as sacred space. Gilders is critical not only of modern scholarly interpretations of sacrifice as symbols. But he also questions those biblical texts that provide "native" explanations for distinct ritual actions, such as the rationale in Leviticus 17:11 that atonement is achieved through blood, which is life.[55]

Martin Modéus uses a similar approach in his study of the communion or peace offering (šĕlāmîm). Due to the ambivalence of the term *sacrifice*, he thinks that its real meaning cannot be determined. Therefore, he understands sacrifice as a means of accentuating social occasions through ritualization. In the Hebrew Bible, for example, the šĕlāmîm offering calls attention to situations in which priests are consecrated or humans express their gratefulness. In addition, the meal associated with this type of sacrifice also connects the participants as a social community.

In general, these scholarly approaches to sacrifice are particularly attentive to communal interactions and observe how the social status of various participants is determined.

Summary and Further Reflections

For several centuries, sacrifice has been the subject of scholarly scrutiny that has yielded a variety of different interpretations. Earlier studies, influenced by Charles Darwin's idea of biological evolution, attempted to explain sacrifice within the broader history of religious development. Likewise, the growing interest in foreign cultures that was the result of European colonialism gave rise to many studies of sacrifice in comparative perspective. It must be mentioned, however, that all comparative treatments are necessarily in danger of importing concepts that are alien to particular cultures and that those comparative treatments were for a long time dominated by the quest for universal theories or the search for one central element. The conclusion by Hubert and Mauss, for instance, that an animal sacrifice could be considered as a sacrifice of the deity, if applied to the religion of ancient Israel and Judah, appears to be without warrant in the texts of the Hebrew Bible.

Despite all this scholarly attention, no consensus has been achieved regarding the meaning of sacrifice; to the contrary, there is an increasing number of different theories on this subject matter. Sacrifices are interpreted as means of identification, substitution, or consecration for humans; they are thought to enable members of social groups to commune with one another and with deities; and so on. Recently, theories that see sacrifice conveying loss or destruction, or that link sacrifice directly with death and murder, have become very prominent. Could this development be influenced by Sigmund Freud's explanation of human culture through negative aspects of the psyche? Whatever the reasons, these theories only affirm the objections raised above, that sacrifice and atonement inevitably connote death, are inherently violent, lead to a problematic image of God, and thus appear to provide the potential for a Christian identity crisis (see pp. 4–8). This could, furthermore, lead to problematic attitudes among Christians, especially if being Christian is understood as *imitatio Christi* in the sense of replicating Christ's example, including his passion and death on the cross. Thus S. Mark Heim warns:

> The spirituality of identification with Jesus' sacrifice can sour in an individual psyche into a questionable brew of morbid fantasies and masochistic eroticism. Ascetic forms of self-mortification are threaded through Christian history . . . for which we would almost certainly seek clinical attention today. . . . Victims of domestic abuse don't need advice to persevere in their suffering as a way of sharing in Christ's redemptive work. . . . The cross should carry a label: this religious image may be harmful to your health.[56]

The problem of sacrifice and atonement needs to be tackled at its root, however, which is Israelite and Judean sacrifice as it is described in detail in the Hebrew Bible. To highlight but two problems with most of the above interpretations and definitions of sacrifice, there is a surprising fixation on animal sacrifice (often called "bloody sacrifice"). Carl Christian Wilhelm Felix Bähr assumes that blood application rites conclude a process of substitutionary incorporation into the Holy and posits the special status of animal sacrifices. In a very similar fashion, Hartmut Gese's concept of atonement also centers on sacrifices "which involve the shedding of blood."[57] Further examples of this opinion can be provided: D. R. Jones states that "sacrifice is pre-eminently bloody sacrifice."[58] Questioning the validity of one general theory of sacrifice, Philip P. Jenson nevertheless singles out the sin offering (which he calls purification offering) and its blood application rites to elucidate the entire sacrificial system of Leviticus.[59] The situation is similar in studies of atonement. Emile Nicole, for instance, when discussing this topic as it relates to the Pentateuch, investigates mostly blood rites that are interpreted in light of Leviticus 17:11.[60]

In contrast, any type of sacrifice from other materials such as plants is usually neglected. Already Hubert and Mauss suggested that it is arbitrary to use the term *sacrifice* only for animal sacrifice and not vegetal materials; they argue that either kind of sacrificial material is destroyed by the altar fire and thus consecrated.[61] Yet how can a theory that focuses on animals and blood application rites provide the rational for the ritual of offering grain, oil, and frankincense? There seems to be more to sacrifice. In a recent publication, Kathryn McClymond observes the tendency of scholars to "exaggerate the importance of killing, characterizing it as the essential feature of sacrificial activity," while they ignore or minimize other ritual activities.[62] Likewise, not every act of killing qualifies as a sacrifice in the Hebrew Bible.

A second problem is the recurrent assumption that, in the Hebrew Bible, identification or substitution occurs between humans and animals. Hartmut Gese, who makes this feature a key aspect of his atonement theory, believes that identification is constituted through the hand-leaning gesture.[63] This, however, remains an argument ex silentio: no Hebrew Bible text actually states anything to that effect.[64]

The Geography of Sacrifice in the Hebrew Bible

Aware of the fact that previous theorizing has been characterized by a rather narrow focus and some questionable assumptions, it is worthwhile for us to investigate sacrifice in the Hebrew Bible anew. As a positive side effect, this endeavor will allow us to become familiar with those parts of the Bible that are usually unknown to most Christians. We will soon notice, however, that sacrifice, when connected to the priestly traditions of the Hebrew Bible, emerges with a different meaning. This has considerable and surprising ramifications for understanding the New Testament metaphor of the sacrifice of Jesus, and thus the concept of atonement.

In an attempt to avoid the pitfalls of previous theories on sacrificial rituals in the Hebrew Bible, the following aspects shall guide my investigation: First, I will not single out one type of sacrifice and claim that it is representative of all other types of sacrifice. I will also avoid paying exclusive attention to animal sacrifices at the expense of sacrifices offered from vegetal materials. Instead, I will study all types of sacrifice specified in the most detailed priestly regulations, namely those in Leviticus 1–7. Second, I will not single out one, or just a few, ritual elements such as blood rites. Instead, I will pay attention to all ritual elements (as much as the limited scope of the present study permits) and particularly to their combination. This approach has recently been called "poly-thetic,"[65] meaning that several ritual activities are interpreted as sequences of connected or progressive events. Third, I shall pay special attention to evidence in the biblical texts that some elements of sacrificial rituals are emphasized while others are not. I shall thus pay attention to indications of how ritual elements are organized hierarchically. And fourth, I shall pay attention to the progression and dynamics of sacrificial rituals as they approach and move through sacred space, eventually arriving at the most holy altar. I shall also study these rituals in relation to the significance of the sanctuary.

Especially with regard to this last aspect, it is suitable to start with a brief sketch of the location of sacrifice; that is, with basic information on, and an outline of, sanctuaries in ancient Israel and Judah. As sacred locations, they form the conceptual and architectonic framework of worship and sacrificial rituals. Without such a sketch, it is neither possible to visualize adequately how the ritual proper unfolds nor to understand its dynamics and significance.

The Sanctuaries of Israel and Judah

Much of the self-understanding of the Hebrew religion was captured in the collection of books of the Hebrew Bible and is still known through those books today. At the core of this religion was the belief in one God. After the story that this God created the world in seven days, the book of Genesis features the story about a garden in Eden (Gen 2:8-25). This is the place where God appears to be in regular contact with the first humans. But it is also the place the first humans have to abandon (3:23-24). From that point on, their contact with God becomes increasingly sporadic. While God still talks to the patriarchs Noah and Abraham, the famous story in which the latter is asked to sacrifice his son Isaac marks the point in the biblical story when an angel intervenes on God's behalf to communicate with even a key protagonist (22:11-12). Soon God, referred to as the "God of heaven" (24:7), is no longer a partner of direct conversation; people are now depicted as addressing God in prayer.

ALTARS AND STONE PILLARS

This development leads to an important question: How and where can God be encountered? On the one hand, altars dedicated to God were built in response to climactic events, for example, after the flood (Gen 8:20-21), or to commemorate special personal experiences with God (12:7; 35:3; in 35:9-15 a stone pillar serves a similar function). Altars thus inscribe past experience with God into the landscape for future reference. Biblical stories relate that people would return to these sacred places with the expectation that they could encounter God there as well.

An altar is, on the other hand, also a place where sacrifices are offered in more or less elaborate ceremonies: Noah offers some of the animals that had survived the flood (Gen 8:20) and Jacob pours out a drink offering on the stone pillar at Bethel (35:14). After the exodus from Egypt, Moses sets up an altar *and* erects stone pillars at Mount Sinai before offering sacrifices; then he conducts the ceremony of the covenant between Israel and God (Exod 24:1-8). From here on, ancient Israel and Judah develop as religious cultures with several sacred places, and the Hebrew Bible contains various references to sacred sites, or sanctuaries (in Hebrew: *qodeš* or *miqdaš*) like those in Gilgal, Shiloh, Shechem, Bethel, Dan, Nob, Ophrah, Hebron, Bethlehem, Arad, Mizpah, or Jerusalem.

For this reason, the Hebrew Bible contains many regulations regarding altars and sanctuaries. These regulations, however, belong to those parts of the Bible that are rather unknown to most Christians. Two examples may suffice. First, many who are familiar with the Ten Commandments, or Decalogue (Exod 20:1-21), are unaware of the fact that this list of religious and ethical standards is immediately followed by what scholars call the Altar Law (20:22-26), one of the oldest cultic decrees in the Bible. The sequence of both texts indicates that, in Israel's legislation, proper morals and proper worship belong together. The Altar Law specifies two basic types of altars for offering sacrifices, namely an altar of earth and

Ancient Israel and Judah. Sanctuaries were located at Dan, Shechem, Shiloh, Bethel, and Hebron, as well as at Jerusalem.

an altar of unwrought stone; it also prohibits that steps be made to approach it and features God's solemn declaration: "In every place where I have my name remembered I will come to you and bless you" (20:24). So here too the altar appears as a location of encounter with God.

Second, many today are familiar with the first half of the book of Exodus, featuring the dramatic story of Israel's liberation from Egypt. Yet not so many are familiar with the remainder of Exodus, which contains elaborate and detailed prescriptions for the tabernacle, Israel's portable sanctuary during the time of their journey through the wilderness (Exod 25–31; 35–40). The sheer amount of text dedicated to these regulations indicates that they were of great religious importance to ancient Israel and Judah.

THE TABERNACLE/"TENT OF MEETING"

The design, function, and purpose of altars and sanctuaries mentioned in the Hebrew Bible are by no means unique, however. Ancient Israel was surrounded by cultures that had long-standing traditions of sanctuaries; modern archaeologists have excavated many of these old sacred sites and buildings in, for example, ancient Babylonia (e.g., in Eridu, Uruk, Ur, Nippur) and Assyria (e.g., in Mari, Calah, Tell Rimah, Tell Brak). Some of these sites have been dated to the early fifth millennium B.C.E. In addition, the Hebrew Bible references a number of temples for pagan gods, for example, the "House of Baal-Berith" (Judg 9:4), the "House of El-Berith" (9:46), the "House of Dagon" (1 Sam 5:2, 5), and the "House of Ashtaroth" (31:10).

Israel's sacred sites and sanctuaries conform more or less to the design and purpose of the sanctuaries of these surrounding cultures. This observation also applies to the biblical narratives about such sites. For example, in the words of Mark K. George, the narrative about Solomon's temple project "is patterned on ancient Near Eastern temple and palace dedication texts (especially Neo-Assyrian texts) in its structure and style."[66] In the ancient world, temples and sanctuaries were generally considered to be places of encounter with the gods. Built as their residences, they were understood to be the point of contact between the earthly and the heavenly realm and were understood to complete the process of the creation of the world.[67]

According to the Hebrew Bible narrative, Israel's first real sanctuary was the so-called tabernacle. This term, derived from Latin *tabernaculum*, means "small hut/tent." The Hebrew name of this sanctuary is "tent of meeting" (Hebrew *'ohel mô'ēd*), conveying two essential aspects: First, it is a portable structure. It could be dismantled and reerected so as to accompany Israel on its wilderness sojourn. Second, the name also indicates that it is the location where Israel could literally meet God. An alternative designation, among others, is "the house of Y<small>HWH</small>" (Exod 23:19), conveying that this tent was God's residence. As mentioned above, the book of Exodus contains the divine prescription to construct this sacred tent under the auspices of Moses, proceeding from the innermost to the outer parts (Exod 25–31). This prescription is followed by the account of the actual construction of this tent, proceeding in opposite direction from the outer to the innermost parts and concluding with its consecration (Exod 35–40).[68] The tent is rectangular and made with curtains supported on poles. It is 30 cubits long[69] (44 feet/13.35 meters), 10 cubits wide (14.7 feet/4.45 meters), and

3 cubits high (4.40 feet/1.34 meters). This structure is separated into a first chamber called the "Holy" (Hebrew: *qodeš*), 20 cubits long (29.4 feet/8.90 meters), and a second chamber called the "Holy of Holies" (Hebrew: *qodeš haqqodašim*), 10 cubits

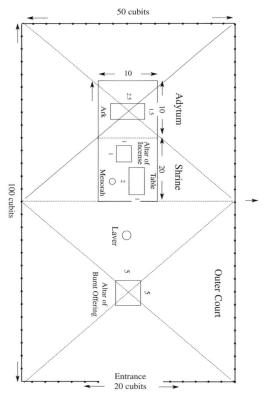

Fig. 1. Ground plan of the tabernacle according to Milgrom, 2004, p. 19; "the Holy" is here labeled the Shrine, and the "Holy of Holies" is called the Adytum.

long (14.7 feet/4.45 meters). A curtain made of blue, purple, and crimson fabric with cherubim worked into it covers the entrance of each chamber. This tent is located in the western half-section of the courtyard that surrounded it. It is oriented on the east-west axis, with its entrance facing "toward the rising sun" (Exod 27:13).[70]

This tent and its courtyard contain a variety of objects. Furnishings and appurtenances in the tent are, as a rule, either entirely made of gold or overlaid with gold; those in the courtyard are made of, or overlaid with, bronze. The Holy of Holies contains the Ark of the Covenant, made

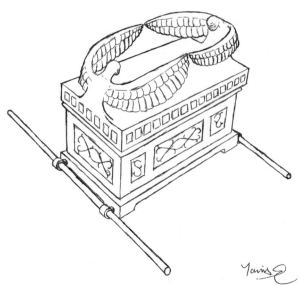

Fig. 2. The Ark of the Covenant; drawing by Yanis Emmanuel Eberhart

of acacia wood and overlaid with gold. It is 2.5 cubits long (3.67 feet/1.11 meters), 1.5 cubits wide (2.20 feet/0.67 meters), and 1.5 cubits high (2.20 feet/0.67 meters). It is covered by the Mercy Seat (Hebrew *kappōret*), a golden lid that also measures 2.5 by 1.5 cubits; its ends feature two statues of cherubim facing each other.

A golden altar is placed in the Holy directly before the curtain of the Holy of Holies. Measuring 1 cubit square (1.47 feet/0.45 meters) and 2 cubits high (2.94 feet/0.90 meters), it is used to burn incense prepared from special ingredients. Further furnishings in this chamber of the tent are the seven-branched lampstand (Hebrew *mēnôrâ*) as well as the table for the bread of the Presence (NRSV, also called the table of showbread).

A rectangular courtyard made with curtains supported on poles surrounds this tent structure. It measures 100 cubits (145 feet/44 meters) by 50 cubits (72 feet/22 meters); its sides are 5 cubits high (7.2 feet/2.20 meters). The courtyard contains the laver made of bronze, placed between the tabernacle tent and the altar of burnt offering. The laver provides the priests with water to wash their hands and feet before entering the tabernacle or before approaching the altar. The main object in the courtyard is the altar of burnt offering. Located in front of the tabernacle entrance, it is square, each side measuring 5 cubits (7.2 feet/2.20 meters) and 3 cubits high (4.4 feet/1.33 meters). It is made of acacia wood overlaid with bronze. The four corners of both the golden and the bronze altar feature horns that probably symbolize the presence and strength of Israel's God. Finally, all of these various objects are equipped with rings through which poles could be inserted for transport.

Other Sanctuaries in Ancient Israel and Judah

When, according to the Hebrew Bible narrative, Israel had conquered the promised land and settled down, several local sanctuaries were being established—or appropriated—from the previous population. Therefore, some of them were strongly connoted with pagan worship and cultic failings or licentious practices (Num 22:41; 1 Kgs 11:7; 12:31; Jer 7:31; Ezek 16:24-43). This is particularly the case with so-called high places (Hebrew *bāmôt*), a name that might suggest that a sanctuary is located on a hill or mountain.[71] Orders were issued to "demolish completely all the places where the nations whom you are about to dispossess served their gods, upon the high mountains, on the hills, and under every green tree" (Deut 12:2; see also Lev 26:30), and periodic reforms were initiated aiming at the centralization of the cult in Jerusalem (2 Kgs 18:4; 23:4-14; 23:8). We may assume that such a "high place" was a small-scale sanctuary, probably featuring at least an altar for offering sacrifices. The fact that it could be mentioned in contrast to a temple (Hebrew: *bajit* or *miqdaš*) indicates that or it most likely lacked an actual sacred building (1 Kgs 3:2).[72]

Other provincial and local sanctuaries of Israel were legitimate at some point in time, but their destinies came to reflect both changes of religious developments and political fate. Therefore, biblical texts contain only scant information on some of these sites. Gilgal, for example, is a town on the eastern border of Jericho (Josh 4:19), even though its exact location remains disputed (Ḥirbet Mefjir? Ḥirbet en-Nitleh?). It was the scene of Israel's first Passover in the land of Canaan (Josh 5:10) and later the site of a local sanctuary where sacrifices were offered (1 Sam 10:8; 15:21). This sacrificial cult was condemned by prophets (Hos 9:15; 12:11; Amos 5:5). Shiloh is a town that has been identified with Tell Seilun, located northeast of Bethel and southeast of Shechem. Shiloh became the base of the tabernacle and the Ark of the Covenant (Josh 18:1; 1 Sam 3:3), indicating the importance of this town during the era of the judges. The priest Eli and his sons served at its regional temple, which was a pilgrimage site periodically visited by family clans to worship and offer sacrifices (1 Sam 1–2). Nevertheless, cultic practices at this temple were criticized as well (2:11-17; see also Judg 18:30-31),[73] and the loss of the Ark as a result of Israel's defeat in battle was a disaster (1 Sam 4:17-22; Ps 78:60-61). Shechem, located approximately sixty-five kilometers north of Jerusalem at the eastern entrance to the pass between Mount Ebal and Mount Gerizim, is already mentioned as a site where Abram stayed on his way to Canaan and built his first altar (Gen 12:6-7). It was later selected as a city of refuge and as a Levitical city (Josh 20:7; 21:21). Fortified by king Jeroboam I, the city became the capital of the kingdom of Israel, the northern part of the land. An earlier temple in Shechem was then destroyed in order to construct an administrative warehouse on its ruins. Bethel, the modern Beitin, is located north of Jerusalem. In the Hebrew Bible, the city is associated with Jacob who, after having a significant dream, built an altar and called the location Beth-El, "house of God" (Gen 28:19; 35:1-7). Recent archaeological excavations, however, point to a previous Canaanite cult of the god El. The fact that, in premonarchic times, the city came to temporarily house the Ark of the Covenant (Judg 20:18-28) suggests that it did have a sanctuary. During the era of the divided kingdoms, Rehoboam made Bethel the capital of the kingdom of Israel. Jeroboam I chose the city for the site of a royal sanctuary, which it was still known as at the time of Amos. Archaeologists have in fact excavated a temple made of stone and several cult objects, but also found evidence that the city was destroyed by the Assyrians during the conquest of Israel in 722 B.C.E.

The Temples in Jerusalem

Moved throughout the territory inhabited by Israel, the tabernacle maintained its status as the main sanctuary and cult site. With these functions, it conveyed that the twelve tribes of Israel all worshiped YHWH, the one God of the "chosen people," at their local sanctuaries. But then political power became consolidated into one kingdom. To create the focal point for a new identity to correspond with this consolidation, King David commissioned, and provided abundant materials for, a future temple project. It was eventually completed by his son Solomon, who reigned from 970 to 930 B.C.E. From that moment on, efforts were made to suspend worship at all local sanctuaries.

The consolidation into one kingdom was supposed to be paralleled by, and supported through, the acknowledgment of one central sanctuary located in the capital. A visible expression of this transfer of religious authority and political power was the transport of the Ark of the Covenant to Jerusalem, where it was supposed to remain (2 Sam 6).

THE HISTORY OF THE TEMPLES

Started in 962 B.C.E. and completed in 955 B.C.E., the construction of Solomon's temple made Jerusalem the most recent city in Israel to have a sanctuary. To dedicate the temple, Solomon ordered that the tabernacle, all of its furnishings, and the Ark be relocated and that the latter be placed in the Holy of Holies (1 Kgs 8:1-13). This temple established Jerusalem as the religious center of Judaism, whence it is known even today as the "Holy City." Solomon's temple also made Jerusalem the political and economic center of Israel and ushered in a thousand-year period during which—with one significant interruption—a temple was located and accessible there. Later, King Josiah of Jerusalem carried out a far-reaching program that further centralized worship in Jerusalem. "The Deuteronomic and Deuteronomistic (Dtr) literature that emerged under Josiah's administration elevated Jerusalem above all other locales in Israel's illustrious covenantal history as the symbol of national religious identity."[74] In 586 B.C.E., when Nebuchadnezzar, king of Babylon, sacked Jerusalem and led the upper class into forced exile, Solomon's temple was destroyed and the temple furnishings and treasures were taken away (2

Kgs 25:8-17; Jer 52:1-27).[75] During the exile, the temple site was in ruins for approximately seventy years. When the Babylonian Empire was, in turn, conquered by Persia in 540 B.C.E., however, the exiled population received permission to return to its homeland. Construction of a second temple began in 538 B.C.E.; after some delay in its completion, its dedication was celebrated twenty-three years later, in the spring of 515 B.C.E. (Ezra 1–6; Hag 1–2). Despite being at first more modest than its predecessor, this edifice developed once more into a religious center of Judaism.[76] It is called "Zerubbabel's Temple" in acknowledgment of the Babylonian Judean who, as chief administrator of the Persian province of *Yehud* (Judea), commanded that the altar in Jerusalem be rebuilt amid ruins and the new temple be erected.

The cause for the initial reluctance of the returning people to build the new temple is the subject of much scholarly dispute. It has been proposed that some might have understood the modesty of the new temple project theologically, so as to indicate that God would not reside there.[77] While this is a possible explanation, a different reason for this reluctance might have been the loss of the Ark of the Covenant. A key object in Solomon's temple, the Ark is never mentioned in connection with Zerubbabel's temple. The Holy of Holies of the new sanctuary was empty (Josephus, *Jewish War* 5:219; Tacitus, *Histories* 5:9).[78] As the Ark represents the actual place of God's presence, its loss would have raised doubts as to whether God would, in fact, return to, and reside in, Jerusalem.[79]

The subsequent political history of the province of *Yehud* continued to be determined by changing allegiances and continuous conflicts. Efforts to Hellenize Palestine, for example, also resulted in a serious disruption of worship at the second temple. In 167 B.C.E., Antiochus Epiphanes, one of the Seleucid kings, had an altar to Zeus erected there, causing the offering of sacrifices for YHWH to cease. This offense triggered the Maccabean revolt, which temporarily restored Judah's political sovereignty and led to the temple's rededication in 164 B.C.E. Politically autonomous, Judah was then ruled by the Hasmonean priestly dynasty until it was conquered by Rome in 63 B.C.E. The Romans initially chose the high priest as governor over the Judeans of Palestine until eventually, in 40 B.C.E., Herod (Greek *Herodēs*) the Great was appointed king. During his reign, from 37 to 4 B.C.E., he commissioned various impressive building projects. Among these was the substantial renovation and enlargement of the second temple, which, for this reason, is generally referred to as the Herodian temple.[80] Begun in 18 B.C.E., most of the work was accomplished within ten years, even though further embellishment continued for decades and was not completed until 63 C.E. Hence the Herodian temple belongs to, and marks the end of, the so-called Second Temple period (515 B.C.E. to 70 C.E.). But this grandiose sanctuary was destroyed in 70 C.E., only seven years later, under the Roman general Titus during the siege of Jerusalem.[81] This event marked the end of a millennium of worship at the temple site that came to epitomize Judaism. Contemporary writers compared the trauma of this destruction to that of Solomon's temple (Josephus, *Antiquities of the Jews* 10:79).[82]

Today, the only remainder of the Herodian temple complex is a segment of its western wall. Known as the "Wailing Wall" or *Kotel* (Hebrew: "wall"), it is still a place of prayer and contemplation in modern Judaism. On the site of the temple, a Muslim sanctuary, the Dome of the Rock (*Qubbet es-Sakhra*), was constructed in 691 C.E.

THE CONSTRUCTION OF THE TEMPLES

Descriptions of the first and second temple of Jerusalem and information on it are featured in biblical (1 Kgs 6:1-38; 7:13-51; 2 Chron 3:1-14; 4:1-10, 19-22; 5:1; Ezra 1:1-6:22; Zech 7:1-8:23) and Jewish sources (Josephus, *Jewish War* 5:184-227; *Mishnah*, tractate *Middot*).[83] The outline and function of both temples resemble more or less that of the tabernacle (see above, pp. 35-39), making some scholars wonder whether the latter may not be considered as a projection of the former. The site of the edifices has been identified as the summit of Mount Moriah (2 Chron 3:1).

Stone, wood, bronze, and gold were among the preferred materials for Solomon's temple. Large blocks of limestone were brought from quarries at Jerusalem to lay the foundation of the temple. Cedars were cut in the forests of Lebanon and imported to Jerusalem by sea; they were used for the building and for the appurtenances, all of which were overlaid with refined gold.

Solomon's temple is described as rectangular, its outside measuring 100 cubits (145 feet/44 meters) by 50 cubits (72 feet/22 meters). The interior measurements are mentioned in 1 Kings 6:2: "And the house that King Solomon built for YHWH: sixty cubits was its length, twenty its width, and thirty cubits its height." These measures refer only to the actual space inside the temple. According to Mordechai Cogan: "These are interior dimensions and do not take into consideration the thickness of either the exterior walls or those that separated the Temple's three rooms. The total of sixty cubits included the main hall and shrine; the porch was measured separately."[84] The actual temple building was surrounded by small auxiliary chambers, 5 cubits high (7.2 feet/2.20 meters) and arranged in three stories. They extended around three sides of the temple except for the entrance side to the east and provided storage room. The porch or vestibule, called *'ûlam* in Hebrew, (Greek: *ailam*) was 10 cubits long (14.5 feet/4.45 meters). It featured two hollow bronze pillars at its front, 18 cubits in height (26.30 feet/8.20 meters), named "Jachin" and "Boaz." A 10-cubit-wide door (14.5 feet/4.45 meters), made of cypress and featuring carvings overlaid with gold, provided entrance to the Holy or main chamber (called *hêkal* in Hebrew, *naos* in Greek). With its length of 40 cubits (58.80 feet/17.80 meters), it was the largest room of the temple and contained several of the furnishings known from the tabernacle, namely the table for the bread of the Presence and the altar of incense. Instead of one seven-branched lampstand, however, it contained "the lampstands of pure gold, five on the south side and five on the north" (1 Kgs 7:49; see also 2 Chron 4:20). Its walls were lined with cedar, while the floor was made of

cypress planks; these were overlaid with·gold. The
windows of the Holy were probably set high in the
walls just below the ceiling. Entrance to the innermost chamber was gained through an olivewood
double door (2 Chron 4:22). Built as a cube 20
cubits long, wide, and high (29.4 feet/8.90 meters),
the floor level of this part of the temple was either
elevated, as would have been the ancient architec-
tural standard for such cellas, or its ceiling was 10
cubits below that of the main temple. Called *dĕbîr*
in Hebrew (the Septuagint does not translate this
term but transcribes it),[85] this chamber is known
in English as "the Holy of Holies," the "most holy
place," or the "adytum." Solomon had the Ark of
the Covenant placed there (1 Kgs 8:1-11). It was
hidden behind the wings of two golden cherubim
that were 10 cubits high (14.7 feet/4.45 meters)
with a 10-cubit wing span.

Solomon's temple was surrounded on all sides
by two courtyards. The inner court, also referred
to as that of the priests (2 Chron 4:9), was separated from the greater court by a wall made of
stone and surmounted by cedar beams. It featured
a number of water basins: one large bronze laver,
10 cubits in diameter (14.7 feet/4.45 meters) and 5
cubits high (7.2 feet/2.20 meters), called the "mol-
ten sea" or "bronze sea" (2 Kgs 25:13; Jer 52:17),
as well as ten smaller bronze lavers. Strangely
enough, the detailed description of the sanctuary
in 1 Kings 6–7 does not mention any altar in the
courtyard, although it would have been the focus
of cultic activities. This is particularly surprising
since later, the story of the temple's consecration
has Solomon stand "before the altar of YHWH"

(1 Kgs 8:22). It also features the following sentence, which concludes with reflections on the insufficient dimensions of that object:

> The king consecrated the middle of the court that was in front of the house of YHWH; for there he offered the burnt offerings and the cereal offerings and the suet pieces of the sacrifices of well-being, because the bronze altar that was before YHWH was too small to receive the burnt offerings and the cereal offerings and the suet pieces of the sacrifices of well-being. (8:64)

This statement indicates that appurtenances had been adjusted to better accommodate changing cult realities.[86] That is why a rather large altar of burnt offering, 20 cubits long and wide (29.4 feet/8.90 meters) and 10 cubits high (14.7 feet/4.45

Fig. 3. The Altar of Burnt Offering; drawing by Yanis Emmanuel Eberhart.

meters), is mentioned in later sources (2 Chron 4:1; 15:8). This altar was accessible through a ramp, not stairs, in accordance with the laws of Exod 20:26 (see above, pp. 32–33). The priest-prophet Ezekiel remembers the postexilic altar as a large stone structure surrounded by a gutter or trench (Ezek 43:13; see also *Mishnah*, tractate *Yoma* 5:6 and tractate *Middot* 3:2).

The first temple, after its destruction in 586 B.C.E., probably determined the ground plan of the second temple through the ruins of its foundation walls. However, the temple of Zerubbabel had been more modest than that of Solomon. This changed toward the end of the second temple's existence, for Zerubbabel's temple is best known in its enlarged and renovated version as the Herodian temple. It gave Judaism a sanctuary that was both of monumental scale and surpassing splendor, making it a visual focal point of the Holy City that was admired even in Rome (Tacitus, *Histories* 5.8.1). In the words of Bart Ehrman,

> The Jewish temple was known to be one of the grandest in the world of antiquity, spoken of with praise and admiration even by those who were not among its devotees. In the days of Jesus, the Temple complex encompassed an area roughly 500 yards by 325 yards. . . . From the outside, its stone walls rose 100 feet from the street, as high as a modern ten-story building. No mortar had been used in its construction; instead, the stones, some of them 50 yards in length, had been carefully cut to fit together neatly. The gates into the temple were 45 feet high by 44 feet wide (with two doors, 22 feet wide, in each); one ancient

source indicates that 200 men were required to
close them each evening.[87]

The actual temple building corresponded
roughly to the dimensions of the previous temples.
Josephus reports, however, that its front had been
enlarged to a square of 100 cubits (145 feet/44
meters) that was entirely covered with gold (*Jewish War* 5:207–8, 222). Major changes were specifically made to its supporting platform and the
courtyards.[88] The trapezoidal temple platform was
expanded and raised to accommodate the fortress Antonia, porticoes, and so on. The courtyard
was surrounded by a double colonnade made in
Roman style. The organization of the courts had
been altered to provide an outer court for gentiles
(alluded to in Rev 11:2) and an inner court exclusively for Judeans. These courts were divided by
stone walls 3 cubits high (4.40 feet/1.34 meters);
they featured pillars with inscriptions in Greek
and Latin that prohibited the access of gentiles to
the inner court (Josephus, *Jewish War* 5:193–94;
Antiquities of the Jews 15:417) in order to prevent defilement of the holy site (Acts 21:28). The
court of the gentiles was the location of money
changers and vendors who offered sacrificial animals and food. The court of the Judeans itself was
subdivided; the platform of each successive court
was raised, accessible through stairs, and surrounded by colonnades. The first court was that
of the women (Josephus, *Jewish War* 5:199). The
smaller, second one was the courtyard surrounding the temple, called the "court of the priests."
Access was also granted to Judean men, who had

to remain behind a wall of partition 1 cubit high (1.47 feet/0.45 meters) (Josephus, *Jewish War* 5:226). From there they could watch the sacrificial

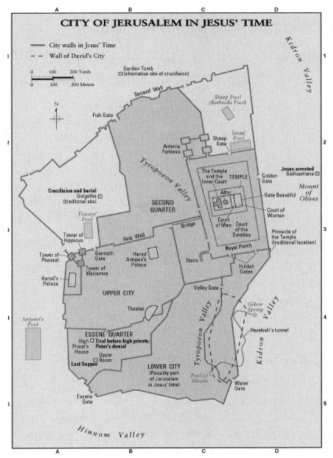

Jerusalem in Jesus' time.

rituals that were performed at the central altar of burnt offering (Matt 5:23-24; see also 23:18-19).

This object was the center of the court of the priests. Josephus describes it as follows: "Before this temple stood the altar, fifteen cubits high, and equal both in length and breadth; each of which dimensions was fifty cubits. The figure it was built in was a square, and it had corners like horns; and the passage up to it was by an insensible acclivity" (*Jewish War* 5:225).

In the temple building, the innermost Holy of Holies remained empty (see above, p. 43). The first or holy chamber featured the same objects as that of Solomon's temple (see above, p. 46). Some of these objects were, upon destruction of the Herodian temple in 70 C.E., brought to Rome by the Roman general Vespasian's army and displayed during a triumph in 71 C.E. The Arch of Titus, erected in 81 C.E. on the *Via Sacra* southeast of the *Forum Romanum*, commemorates this procession for propaganda purposes. Depicting the seven-branched lampstand as well as the table of showbread, this arch features the only contemporary graphic representation of objects from the Jerusalem sanctuary.

The Significance and Importance of Sanctuaries

Sanctuaries in ancient Israel and Judah were places of public gathering, celebration, and worship. It should be mentioned, however, that people approaching such sacred sites for pilgrimages or other purposes would have proceeded to the sacred precinct to worship and offer sacrifices.

They could not enter the actual temple building. Yet different cultic realities portrayed in the Hebrew Bible show that even the approach to the courtyards became gradually more restrictive. A preexilic narrative set at the temple or sanctuary (Hebrew *hêkāl*) in Shiloh presupposes that a woman like Hannah could advance to the door of the temple for prayer (1 Sam 1:9-10). In contrast to this, roughly one millennium later the organization of sacred space at the Herodian temple no longer allowed Judean women to proceed to the courtyard that immediately surrounded the temple proper. Their access was limited to the court of the women, from which the worship activities performed by the priests were not even visible. Only Judean men had the right to enter the innermost court and watch the priests at the altar of burnt offering. It appears, however, that even this limited visual access was unusual by ancient Near Eastern cult standards, which were even more restrictive.[89] When the Gospel according to Mark mentions that Jesus "entered the temple and began to drive out those who were selling and those who were buying in the temple" (11:15; see also John 2:13-16), then the term *temple* (Greek: *hieron*) refers in a wider sense to the entire temple complex. This scene envisages the courtyard of the Gentiles at the Herodian temple.

It is worth mentioning that synagogues and churches of biblical and postbiblical times are conceptually different from temples in antiquity because they allow the congregation to access the actual building. This difference is, for instance, conveyed in the very term *synagogue*, which means literally "meeting, assembly" (the Greek verb *syn-agein*, "to gather, assemble," is a compound of *syn*, "with, together," and *agein*, "to lead, bring").

We may assume, though, that the temple proper, in all of these cult periods, was exclusively reserved for priests, and even they entered only in order to perform their duties. For example, Eli, the priest at the local sanctuary of Shiloh, routinely sat "on the seat beside the doorpost of the temple of YHWH" (1 Sam 1:9), but not inside it. At the tabernacle and at the first and second temple in Jerusalem, all priests were obliged to perform ablution rites before entering the Holy (Exod 30:20). The Holy of Holies, however, could only be accessed by the high priest, and only once per year, on the Day of Atonement (*yôm hakkippurîm*) on the tenth day of the month of Tishri (Lev 16:29).

The reason for such restricted access is that the sanctuary was considered the earthly dwelling place of God; hence its designation as "house of God/YHWH" (e.g., 1 Sam 3:15; 2 Sam 12:20; 1 Kgs 8:10-11; 9:10, 15; 2 Kgs 12:10-18; 1 Chron 28:12-13; 2 Chron 24:18; see also 2 Kgs 19:37; John 2:16).[90] This designation can be seen as entirely analogous to a human domicile: "the house of YHWH and the houses of the king" (2 Chron 28:21). The prophet Jeremiah, while standing in a temple gate, delivered a warning on behalf of God: "Amend your ways and your doings, then I will dwell with you in this place" (Jer 7:3). That the God of Israel entered and was present at the sanctuary is clearly conveyed when, during the dedication ceremonies of the first temple, a cloud representing the divine presence filled the sacred edifice

(1 Kgs 8:10-11). In his subsequent prayer, Solomon says that God "would dwell in thick darkness" (8:12), referring to the total obscurity of the Holy of Holies, which had no windows (see also Ps 97:2). This concept is similarly articulated for the portable tent of meeting. God initially orders, "Make me a sanctuary that I may dwell among them" (Exod 25:8). Upon the completion and consecration of the tabernacle, the divine cloud "covered the tent of meeting, and the glory of YHWH filled the dwelling" (Exod 40:34).[91] Therefore, both the tabernacle and the temple of ancient Israel were equipped with objects that were actually furnishings, such as lamps and tables. They, too, represent the temple as the divine household. Ancient Israel and Judah shared this concept with other ancient Near Eastern religions, as has already been noted above (p. 35).

The Hebrew Bible, while prohibiting any image of God, is nevertheless at times very specific regarding the precise locus of God's presence. Thus the detailed instructions regarding the construction of the Ark of the Covenant conclude with the following statement: "You shall put the Mercy Seat on the top of the Ark; and in the Ark you shall put the covenant that I shall give you. There I will meet with you, and from above the Mercy Seat, from between the two cherubim that are on the Ark of the Covenant, I will deliver to you all my commands for the Israelites" (Exod 25:21-22; see also Num 7:89). Likewise, the designation "the Ark of the Covenant of YHWH of hosts who is enthroned above/between the cherubim" (1 Sam 4:4; see also 2 Sam 6:2; 2 Kgs 19:15; Ps 80:2; 99:1) presupposes that God hovers above the *kappōret*, the Ark's golden cover (see above, p. 38). This is equally conveyed when the Ark is called a "footstool of YHWH" (1 Chron 28:2; Ps 99:5; 132:7).[92] The utmost sanctity of the innermost chamber of the sanctuary is, therefore, due to the presence of the Holy God of Israel. Despite such specific ideas about God's dwelling in the earthly sanctuary, no conflict was perceived with the thought of God's simultaneous presence in heaven (Ps 11:4; see also Matt 23:21-22).

While such specific ideas about God's presence might seem strange to postmodern people, it may be mentioned that contemporary Jewish and Christian worship space is to some extent related to these ancient concepts and conveys similar ideas about sanctity. The tripartite outline of ancient Near Eastern temple complexes, which consisted of a public courtyard, a chamber for priests, and a chamber exclusively reserved for the deity, became the conceptual paradigm for later synagogues and churches, in which the congregation is typically seated in one area; the rabbi, priest, or pastor officiates and proclaims in a second area; and a third space is reserved for the presence of God, which it indicates through features such as the "Torah ark" (a cabinet for the sacred Torah scrolls in a synagogue), the "tabernacle" (a cabinet for the consecrated eucharistic hosts in some churches), or a cross. These three areas are frequently divided: usually elevated, the space of the officiating minister is accessible via steps; sometimes hidden behind a screen or curtain, the space of the divine presence is out of bounds for the common person.

It is clear that the priestly portrayal of God as "enthroned" above the *kappōret* envisions a heavenly king who has the power to protect Israel on the one hand, but on the other hand also to judge it. God's kingdom was imagined to be of universal scope; God was acclaimed "as king in Israel and king over all of creation, over all other gods and over all the nations."[93] Therefore, God's presence in the temple was supposed to bestow peace (Hebrew *šālôm*) upon the land (Ps 29:10-11).[94] When Israel and ancient Judah offered sacrifices at God's altar, the hope was alive that God would remember the chosen people and bless them according to the promise of the Altar Law (Exod 20:22-26; see above, p. 33).

Yet in antiquity, a sanctuary was never exclusively a religious institution, and people did not only visit it to encounter God. A sanctuary was also important for other reasons. Most national sanctuaries had economic and social importance as well since they housed the national treasury and were, given their sometimes monumental dimension and great splendor, objects of pride and identification for the people. The following statement concisely captures the many facets of this importance: "In modern-day parlance, the shrine complex would be like having the 'IRS, Supreme Court, National Cathedral, and CitiBank' all rolled up into one multipurpose institution."[95] That the temple was considered an object of identification was, on the one hand, of paramount significance during most of the Second Temple period, when Judah had lost its political sovereignty. Zerubbabel's temple, on the other hand, became an immediate location of political power because, during Persian and Roman hegemony, the high priest was given jurisdiction over the province of Judah. Finally, it has been noted that the sanctuary may be regarded as a microcosm of the social characteristics of its surrounding culture. According to Mark K. George, studies of the tabernacle ground plan and of its liturgical ceremonies expose characteristics of the society itself. "What analysis of tabernacle social space reveals are the hidden social codes and systems that situate Israel within the very fabric and order of creation. Those codes and systems reflect the social ideas, preferences, concerns, priorities, and other anxieties of the Priestly writers."[96]

With this spectrum of aspects and features, the temple in Jerusalem came to epitomize ancient Judaism. Therefore its destruction by the Romans in 70 C.E. was a highly traumatic event. How did Judaism respond to this catastrophe? How has Judaism grappled with the fact that the temple has never been rebuilt? Half a millennium earlier, after the destruction of Solomon's temple, the situation of the exiled people in Babylonia required that new social paradigms be created. While the Hebrew Bible presents the tabernacle as a precursor to Solomon's temple, Mark K. George argues that the need of those in exile generated the imagination of a mobile sanctuary not limited to one specific location.[97]

It can be asked whether such an analysis of the significance of the tabernacle sanctuary might apply mutatis mutandis to the narrative depiction of the second temple after its destruction as well. It continued to serve as a point of reference for

Judaism and the emerging Christian movement. Its memory lives on through the "virtual reality" based on literary works such as the Bible, the books of the Qumran community (particularly the *Temple Scroll*, 11QT),[98] Josephus, and rabbinic literature. They all provide detailed descriptions of the temple, including its ground plan, splendor, worship, and theological significance. Its meaning for early Christianity is evident in all four New Testament Gospels, particularly in the Gospel according to Luke. Key events take place in the temple, such as the annunciation of the birth of John the Baptist (Luke 1:11-20) or of the future prominence of Jesus (Luke 2:25-38). Jesus himself teaches in the temple precincts, first at twelve years of age (Luke 2:42-51), and later also during his ministry (Mark 12:35; John 7:14, 28). The fact that charges which eventually lead to the death of Jesus (Mark 14:58; 15:29) have to do with the controversial scene known as the "cleansing of the temple" (11:15-19) likewise attests to the importance of the temple for Judaism. In addition, the tabernacle or the temple in Jerusalem is evoked as the dwelling place of God when Christ is introduced as the incarnate word that literally "tented among us" (John 1:14), when Jesus talks about his body being the temple (John 2:21), or when Christians are called "temple of God" (1 Cor 3:16-17; 6:19; Eph 2:21).[99]

Judaism and early Christianity remembered specifically the sacrificial cult that was celebrated at the temple because sacrifices constituted an essential part of worship at the temple. In the sixth century B.C.E., sacrifices were still offered in the ruins of Solomon's temple, and sacrifices were also offered in the ruins of the Herodian temple until the Bar Kochba revolt (132–36 C.E.);[100] among other things, this revolt aimed at reestablishing the sacrificial cult.[101] Rabbinic Judaism still visualized this cult and discussed its features as if it never ceased. According to Gary A. Anderson, "This 'as if' quality of rabbinic speech continues to influence readers of rabbinic literature until the present day."[102] Sacrificial rituals and images were, however, also applied in early Christianity, for example in ethical passages of New Testament letters and to articulate the importance of the mission of Jesus.

The Meaning of Different Sacrifices in the Hebrew Bible

The core component of the worship at all sanctuaries in antiquity was sacrifice. Sacrifices were brought to the deity who resided at the sanctuary. In the Hebrew Bible, the detailed account of the construction and dedication of the portable tabernacle, or "tent of meeting," which concludes with the explicit statement that the glory of YHWH enters it (Exod 40:34, see above, p. 55), is therefore immediately followed by sacrificial rituals in Leviticus 1–7. This sequence conveys that sacrifice is what has to be done at the sanctuary. It also means that sacrifices are set within the imaginary environment of the tabernacle from which, according to Leviticus 1:1, YHWH speaks to Moses to instruct him on the matter of sacrifices.

For today's readers of these sacrificial rituals, however, and especially for the purposes of this investigation, at least three problems are evident. First, given that neither Judaism nor Christianity still practices sacrificial rituals, "nothing could seem more distant from our modern lives than a system of animal sacrifice."[103] This problem is even more acute when one realizes that the biblically commanded sacrifices were to take place at specific sacred sites that no longer exist. Second, these ancient descriptions of sacrificial action provide no straightforward or concise definition of sacrifice. Instead, the reader encounters detailed rituals that offer only little information on what they mean. It is up to the readers—who are not participants in these rituals—to draw further conclusions. Third, it is not a matter of just one sacrifice; no fewer than five different types of sacrifice are distinguished in Leviticus 1–7. Thus, sacrifice in the Hebrew Bible—as in all ancient Near Eastern religions—appears as a multifaceted phenomenon that comprises not only animal sacrifices but also involves offerings of grain and other vegetal substances.

For this reason, sacrifice remains a much-disputed topic, as the previous survey of scholarly theories suggests (see above, pp. 14–25). For the purpose of providing a well-grounded analysis of sacrifices in the Hebrew Bible, I turn next to examine in detail the pertinent core text in Leviticus 1–7 and to investigate all five types of sacrifice mentioned there, namely the burnt offering, the cereal offering, the well-being sacrifice, the sin offering, and the guilt offering.[104] I shall assume that the priestly texts were intentionally shaped to provide contemporaries with the necessary instructions to offer sacrifices. In the words of Ithamar Gruenwald, "the cultic environment of the sanctuary leaves nothing to chance or to non-systemic performance. Indeed, it activates a more sophisticated systematization of rituals, in which clearly specified names and functions play a major role."[105]

The Burnt Offering

The ritual of the burnt offering is featured in Leviticus 1:1-17; additional information for the priestly service is contained in 6:1-6. In Hebrew, this type of sacrifice is called *'ōlâ*, which means "rising/ascending (offering)"; the Septuagint has a total of eight Greek equivalents, of which *holokautōma* and *holokautōsis,* "complete burning," are the most frequent ones. All terms imply that this offering is burned in its entirety. The first ritual to be featured is that of a bull (Lev 1:3-9):

> If the offering is a burnt offering from the herd, he[106] shall offer a male without blemish; he shall bring it to the entrance of the tent of meeting, for acceptance on his behalf before YHWH. He shall lean his hand on the head of the burnt offering that it may be acceptable on his behalf to atone for him. He shall slaughter the bull before YHWH; and Aaron's sons, the priests, shall bring the blood and dash the blood against all sides of the altar that is at the entrance of the tent of meeting. He shall flay the burnt offering and cut it into its parts. The sons of the priest Aaron shall put fire

on the altar and arrange wood on the fire. Aaron's sons the priests shall arrange the parts, with the head and the suet, on the wood that is on the fire on the altar; but its entrails and its legs shall be washed with water. Then the priest shall burn the whole on the altar as a burnt offering; [this is] an offering by fire, a pleasing odor for YHWH.

This ritual requires, first, that the person who intends to offer a burnt offering chooses an appropriate animal—a bull, a sheep, a goat, a pigeon, or a dove. Then the person is to bring the live animal to the sanctuary. The purpose is "acceptance on his behalf before YHWH" (Lev 1:3) and thus presupposes that the God of Israel is now in residence at this location and can be encountered there.

At the sanctuary, the ritual consists of seven distinct components that are similar to most of the other types of sacrifice. First, the offerer has to lean (not "lay") one hand on the animal's head (1:4); the Hebrew verb *smk* implies pressure, as in Judges 16:29, where Samson leans against the central pillar of a house in order to make it collapse.[107] The biblical text does not explain what the hand-leaning gesture means. Therefore, scholars have discussed several possible explanations. That it implies the transferral of sin from the human to the sacrificial animal is unlikely, since a burnt offering does not necessarily presuppose that the offerer has sinned; this kind of sacrifice can also be offered as an expression of joy or gratitude toward God. In addition, the transferral of sin is associated with the imposition of two hands on the scapegoat (Lev 16:21); this ritual, however, is not a cultic sacrifice but an elimination rite. Furthermore, in the context of sacrificial rituals, only one hand is imposed, not two. A different explanation of the hand-leaning gesture is that the offerer identifies with the animal, but it is unclear what significance personal identification could have for this type of sacrifice. Therefore, the most likely explanation is that the offerer declares ownership of the animal before the officiating priests continue to handle it in subsequent ritual actions. Correspondingly, the note that the burnt offering "may be acceptable on his behalf to atone [Hebrew *kipper*] for him" (Lev 1:4) assures that the desired effect of bringing this sacrifice falls back on the person who declared ownership through the hand-leaning gesture.[108]

The second ritual element is the slaughter of the animal, to be carried out by the offerer (Lev 1:5). The Hebrew verb *šḥt* implies that the throat of the animal is slit with a knife. As this technique was generally used for animal slaughter and well known in ancient nomadic cultures, no further information on this procedure is provided in any Hebrew Bible text on ritual.[109] The location of animal slaughter is not the altar of burnt offering, which is considered most sacred, but instead the less sacred "outer half of the Tabernacle court between the entrance of the enclosure and the altar."[110] According to Leviticus 1:11, goats and sheep are to be slaughtered north of the altar. In his temple vision, Ezekiel likewise describes eight tables for animal slaughter that were installed north of the altar in the vestibule of the gate (Ezek 40:39-41).[111] It is, finally, worth mentioning that no interpretive comment appears in connection with the act of slaughter.

The third ritual element is carried out by the officiating priests. They bring the animal blood to the altar of burnt offering, located in the court-yard in front of the tent of meeting, and dash it against all sides of the altar (Lev 1:5). The blood then flows into the gutter surrounding the altar (see above, p. 49) and drains into the ground. No explanation is offered for this action anywhere in the Hebrew Bible. It may be assumed, however, that it had the purpose of returning the animal's life, which was considered to be in its blood (Lev 17:11), to a sacred site and thus to God, the giver of life. This third element introduces the phase of apportionment that, according to Kathryn McCly-mond, "refers to the division of a single offer-ing unit into multiple pieces or portions and the assignation of these portions to specific ritual par-ticipants."[112] The blood, separated from the animal body, is therefore apportioned to God.

With the fourth step of the ritual, the scene shifts back to the offerer at the entrance of the enclosure, who is to flay the burnt offering (Lev 1:6). If the act of slaughter already seemed to carry some connotations of profane acts of slaughter for the purpose of preparing a meal, this step and sub-sequent ones definitely do so. Flaying an animal was a well-known activity in ancient nomadic cultures and required no further explanation. The animal hide was the only part of the sacrificial animal not to be burned; eventually the officiat-ing priest received it (Lev 7:8). The offerer then dismembers the sacrificial animal.

With the fifth ritual action, the attention reverts to the priests, who literally "give" fire on the altar of burnt offering (Lev 1:7). The ritual does not imagine that the fire be kindled anew since it is to burn continually (Lev 6:12-13; MT, LXX 6:5-6).[113] Instead, the priests stoke the altar fire by arranging wood on it. In a sixth step, they wash the legs and entrails and arrange the parts of the animal with its head, suet, entrails, and legs, in short all parts of the sacrificial animal except for its hide, on the wood that is on the altar (Lev 1:8-9). Jacob Milgrom comments: "It is assumed that prior to this rite the meat was salted."[114]

The seventh ritual element is the burning of the entire sacrificial material that is on the altar, articulated through the Hebrew verb *qtr* (*hiph'il*: Lev 1:9).[115] This verb always denotes burning in a cultic context and is, therefore, restricted to burning on an altar for the purpose of worshiping God (Exod 29:13; Lev 16:25). This rite is accompanied by further terms: "[This is] an offering by fire, a pleasing odor for YHWH." The burning rite concludes the ritual activity of the burnt offering.

The ritual prescription in Leviticus 1:3-9 presents many details of the ritual activity carried out either by the offerer or by the priests; yet this is not its sole focus. It also features various interpretive comments that inform the ancient Israelite who was about to offer a burnt offering—as well as subsequent readers of the text—about the effect of particular components of ritual activity. Regarding the information in this ritual prescription, therefore, we can distinguish between descriptive or prescriptive (action-oriented) and interpretive (meaning-oriented) passages. The existence of the latter evinces the importance of establishing an interpretive framework when reading sacrificial rituals.

The first of these interpretive comments appears early in the ritual instructions: When the offerer chooses the right sacrificial animal and brings it to Israel's sanctuary, then the sacrifice accomplishes "acceptance" on his behalf "before YHWH" (1:3). The next sentence, on the hand-leaning gesture, concludes with two interpretive phrases: "It [the sacrifice] may be acceptable on his behalf to atone [Hebrew *kipper*] for him" (1:4). The concluding burning rite also features two interpretive comments: "an offering by fire, a pleasing odor for YHWH" (1:9). What do these comments convey?

The term "offering by fire," Hebrew *'iššeh*,[116] refers to a process of metamorphosis of the sacrificial substance offered by a human being. It conveys the idea that the altar fire does not just destroy this material.[117] According to the cognitive framework of ancient Israel and many other ancient Near Eastern cultures, the altar fire instead changes the sacrificial material and transforms it into a new, ethereal essence. The term "offering by fire" thus indicates that the sacrificial material belongs no longer to the earthly but now to the heavenly or transcendent sphere. The second interpretive comment is the phrase "a pleasing odor [Hebrew *rêaḥ-nîḥôaḥ*] for YHWH."[118] It articulates the effect of the burning rite on God, and therefore of the sacrifice at large. It encapsulates how the transformed sacrificial material rises upward in the form of smoke; it is this characteristic movement

that is captured by the Hebrew term *'ōlâ* ("rais-
ing/ascending"). The sacrifice is thus being trans-
ported to God, who perceives its odor and accepts
it. The modern reader of the Bible might find such
an anthropomorphic view of God strange and perhaps offensive. God smells sacrifices? However, the
Hebrew Bible clearly describes how God perceives
the burnt offerings that Noah sacrifices after the
flood: "And when YHWH smelled the pleasing odor,
YHWH said in his heart, 'I will never again curse
the ground because of humankind'" (Gen 8:21).[119]
One might describe the effect of this sacrifice as
propitiation of God.

Hence, the two interpretive comments at the
conclusion of the ritual of the burnt offering
(Lev 1:9) express the way in which the sacrificial
substance is transformed by fire and ascends to
heaven as smoke to be perceived by God. Both
interpretive terms help us to understand the previous ones about acceptability and atonement (1:3-
4). These state that, on the one hand, the correct
choice of the sacrificial animal matters because in
the end, the sacrifice is for God; thus, it should be
of the highest quality. God may accept the sacrifice offered by humans, but it is possible that
God may not accept it if is of inferior quality (Lev
22:18-25; Mal 1:12-14).

On the other hand, the sacrificial cult is about
encountering God. While God may at times appear
to be very close or familiar, God can also be "the
other" who is not only unknown and unfamiliar
but also even threatening. For this reason, Moses
prepares for his encounters with God through
signs of deference such as taking off his shoes and

covering his face (Exod 3:5-6).[120] The sacrificial cult presupposes that God and humans live in different worlds. They are also separate because God is holy while humans are not, and because God's status is infinitely higher than that of humans. After all, the God of ancient Israel and Judah is being worshiped at the tabernacle or temple as a heavenly king (see above, p. 57). Given this difference in status, how can humans ever meet God? The sacrificial cult mediates between these separate worlds and allows humans to appear before God. The term *atonement* is a very complex concept, but its outcome is such a mediated encounter that it might, under certain circumstances, imply the expiation of human sin and impurity.

In the ancient Near East, every encounter between parties of different status obliges the lower party to bring a token of homage that indicates due respect and deference for the superior party. In most modern cultures, by the way, this cultural norm is still in effect; everybody who has ever assisted at a visit of a high political representative like, for instance, the president of the country knows that a standard custom for such an encounter is the presentation of gifts, which are, in the end, tokens of reverence. A sacrifice is such a token. This is conveyed by the term "offering [Hebrew *qorbān*] for YHWH" that the priestly texts employ as a general term for sacrifice (e.g., Lev 1:2-3, 10, 14; 2:1, 4; 3:1; 4:23, 28, 32; 7:38). The English translation of *qorbān* as "offering" corresponds to, and is perhaps based on, the Septuagint rendering *dōron*—"offering, present."[121] Outside of the priestly texts, another general term for sacrifice is *minḥâ*. In the story of Cain and Abel, for example, *minḥâ* refers to both Cain's offering from "the fruits of the soil" and to the portions that Abel offers of the firstlings of his flock (Gen 4:3-5). It is instructive that this term occurs as well in non-cultic contexts, where it has the meaning of "gift, tribute," which expresses political submission to a party of superior status.[122] With this meaning, *minḥâ* is partially equivalent to *qorbān*. These terms convey two main aspects about ritual sacrifice: First, sacrificial animals are objects of material value. In a nomadic culture, bulls, sheep, and goats are prime examples of personal property; the size of the herd constitutes somebody's "financial" standing. This understanding still prevails in rabbinic Judaism; Rabbi Nehemiah said, "Sufferings are more acceptable than sacrifices, because sacrifices affect a man's money, but sufferings affect his body."[123] Therefore, the term *qorbān* has monetary connotations, and the sacrifice of an animal as an "offering for YHWH" amounts to material loss.[124]

Second, however, this material loss is not all that sacrifice is about. The basic structure of sacrifice is that of exchanging offerings. Israel is always the partner who receives in this exchange from God, who has gracefully given Israel its identity and provided the resources of creation (1 Chron 29:14-17). Cultic sacrifice is then seen as a segment in the structure of reciprocal exchange that aims at establishing or confirming a relationship with God.[125] This reciprocity, however, does not imply that the offerings of either side compare in size or value. Valerio Valeri explains the difference of the offerings as reflecting the status of the giver: "The value of the thing given is inversely proportional to that of the giver. In other words, for a god, giving much is giving little; for man, giving little is giving much. Hence man's small gift to the god is as valuable as god's big gift to man, but at the same time this equivalence of the gifts signifies and establishes the nonequivalence of the givers, of god and man."[126]

The term *qorbān*, however, implies yet a third aspect. Derived from the Hebrew root *qrb* (*hiph'il*), "to bring near, make approach," the literal meaning of *qorbān* is "that which is brought near to YHWH." The term thus references the dynamics of the entire process of sacrifice, which, in fact, is a gradual movement toward and through sacred space and an approach to God: It commences at the house of the offerer, from which the appropriate sacrificial material must be brought to God's sanctuary; it continues with the actual ritual, which moves step by step from the outside of the sacred precincts to its center; it concludes in the burning rite, which aims at transforming the sacrificial substance and transporting it to God.[127] Hebrew *qorbān* is thus a powerful term that comprehensively conveys the dynamics of a sacrificial ritual. Unfortunately, these aspects are mostly lost in the common English rendering "offering."

Hence, the various interpretive comments in the context of the burnt offering ritual in Leviticus 1:3-9 communicate important insights into the contemporary understanding of sacrifices in ancient Judaism. The terms "offering by fire" and "pleasing odor" communicate an emphasis on the burning rite on the altar. Understood as transformation of sacrificial material and its transport to God, these comments suggest that the burning constitutes the nature of the burnt offering as an "offering for YHWH." As this offering is an appropriate token of reverence, humans can encounter God at the sanctuary and be accepted; if necessary, God grants atonement (Hebrew *kipper*).

In the ritual of the burnt offering, all parts of the sacrificial animal (except for its hide) are apportioned to God. While the blood is being dashed against the altar, these parts are all burned on the altar in the courtyard. This burning rite is clearly the essential feature of the burnt offering ritual. Its emphasis is evident considering the sheer amount of text dedicated to it: the Hebrew text of the entire ritual in Leviticus 1:3-9 consists of eighty-nine words. Of these, forty-five words deal with the actions prior to the burning rite; and forty-four words are dedicated to the burning rite and related activities, that is, the stoking of the fire, the arranging of the individual parts of the sacrificial animal on the altar, and the associated interpretive terminology.

The dominance of the burning rite is further evidenced as we study the remainder of the ritual regulations on the burnt offering in Leviticus 1. After describing the burnt offering of the bull, the text continues with that from the flock, that is, "from either the sheep or from the goats" (1:10), and concludes with that from birds, namely, "from the turtledoves or from the pigeons" (1:14). It is interesting to note that, while these rituals are once more recounted in great detail, neither the hand-leaning gesture nor the interpretive comments regarding acceptability and atonement found in 1:3, 4 are mentioned. Scholars generally assume that the hand-leaning nevertheless occurred (and might have been implied in the peculiar phrasing of Leviticus 1:4) and that a sacrifice from the flock or from birds is acceptable and atones as well.[128] It is rather telling, however, that the detailed description of what is to be placed on the altar for the burning rite and the related interpretive comments "offering by fire" and "pleasing odor for YHWH" recur in full length in each instance (1:12-13; 1:17). This indicates again the importance of the burning rite.

This crucial ritual activity is emphasized even further in the priestly texts. The "Torah of the burnt offering" that contains exclusive instructions for the priests is featured in Leviticus 6:8-13 (MT, LXX 6:1-6). It contains regulations such as: "The burnt offering shall remain on the hearth upon the altar throughout the night until the morning, while the fire on the altar shall be kept burning" (Lev 6:9; MT, LXX 6:2); "the fire on the altar shall be kept burning; it must not go out. . . . A perpetual fire shall be kept burning on the altar; it must not go out" (Lev 6:12-13; MT, LXX 6:5-6). These instructions demonstrate that special care for the altar fire is of prime importance for this type of sacrifice. The reason might be that this fire and the smoke ascending from it made God's presence at the sanctuary visible. In the sanctuary of some modern churches, God's presence is still indicated by a permanently lit candle or lamp above the altar.

But the burning rite is, moreover, of importance for the entire sacrificial cult. It is part of
all five different types of sacrifice in the priestly
description of the cult, as the following overview
will show. A final accentuation of the burning rite
occurs in the story about the official inauguration of the sacrificial cult at the tabernacle (Lev 9).
It portrays Aaron, the high priest, as he prepares
various different types of sacrifice, yet does not
light any fire on the altar. After the preparations
are completed, the climax of the cult inauguration
is marked by the "fire from before YHWH" (9:24)
that suddenly appears and consumes the sacrificial substances on the altar. The final event indicates that Israel's sacrificial cult has been accepted
by God.

We have seen that, because the burning rite
transforms sacrifices into an ethereal quality
and transports them to God, sacrifices are called
"offerings to YHWH" in priestly texts. This aspect is
connected with another one, namely that of food.
A comprehensive view of the burnt offering in
Leviticus 1 shows that all of the sacrificial materials such as a bull, a sheep or goat, or a bird, are
comestible goods. Moreover, other aspects of ritual
activities belong to the realm of food and food
preparation, specifically slaughtering, flaying, and
cutting in pieces. In addition, the meat of the sacrifice is to be salted. According to other texts, sacrifices are to be presented at the "house of God"
on an altar that is frequently called "hearth" or
"table" (Lev 6:9; MT, LXX 6:2; Ezek 41:22; 44:16;
Mal 1:12). Therefore, it is not surprising that sacrifices can explicitly be called "food" or "bread"

of God (Num 28:2, 24). The idea cannot be denied that sacrifices in ancient Israel and early Judaism were considered and described as offerings in the context of a meal.[129]

It is, however, a misunderstanding to assume that the God of Israel needs to be nourished. The purpose of describing sacrifices as meals is rather that of maintaining relationships and indicating honor. On the one hand, meals and banquets in the ancient Near East were typical occasions for people to socialize, to confirm their own status, and acknowledge that of others. In modern Mediterranean culture (for example, Italy and France), a lot of relationships are still forged over the course of a dinner that can easily last between three and five hours. In this regard, such meals are the strict opposite of the contemporary western fast-food culture, which is limited to the exclusive purpose of food intake. In the Hebrew Bible, the symbolism of sacrifices as "food" or "bread" conveys that the divine host invites humans for the purpose of establishing lasting relations. On the other hand, both the type and quality of the food that humans present convey their acknowledgment of God's superior status as a divine king. Hospitality is, therefore, a significant interpretive frame of sacrificial rituals in the Hebrew Bible.[130]

The Cereal Offering

The ritual of the cereal offering is featured in Leviticus 2:1-16; additional instructions are found in 6:14-23 (MT, LXX 6:7-16). In Hebrew, this type of sacrifice is called *minḥâ*. As mentioned previously, *minḥâ* can, as a comprehensive cultic term, mean "offering" in general; in noncultic contexts it has the meaning of "tribute." In Leviticus 2, *minḥâ* occurs in a cultic setting but with a more specific meaning: it is the technical term for a sacrifice prepared from vegetal substances, not animals. Therefore, its standard English translation is either "grain offering" or "cereal offering."[131]

Much of traditional and modern scholarship takes little notice of the cereal offering. Kathryn McClymond notes: "The dominant theorists—Hubert, Mauss, Burkert, and Girard—virtually ignore vegetal sacrifice in their work, literally reducing vegetal offerings to footnotes."[132] Her statement is corroborated by the previous survey of scholarship (see above, pp. 14–26). McClymond continues that this disregard is not warranted by the available texts: "Vegetal oblations appear prominently in the ritual literature of many sacrificial traditions, including the Vedic and Jewish traditions, and it is important to emphasize that these vegetal offerings are not just substitutes for animal offerings but act as distinct offerings in their own right."[133] It is, therefore, appropriate to study the ritual of the cereal offering in the ancient Judean cult as it is described in Leviticus 2:1-3.

> When a person brings a cereal offering for Yнwн, the offering is to be of fine flour. The person shall pour oil on it and put frankincense on it, and bring it to Aaron's sons the priests. The priest shall take a handful of the fine flour and oil, together with all the frankincense, and burn this as a memorial portion on the altar; [this is] an

offering by fire, a pleasing odor for Y<small>HWH</small>. The rest of the cereal offering shall be for Aaron and his sons; it is a most holy part of the offerings by fire for Y<small>HWH</small>.

The most characteristic attribute of this sacrifice is its vegetal substance. It can be prepared from raw or unprocessed grains of cereal and is accompanied by oil and frankincense, a fragrant gum resin that is as rare as it is expensive. The subsequent ritual instructions describe a cake that is baked in the oven (Lev 2:4) or toasted (2:5-6), or that is of fried grains (2:7); from first-ripe fruits, it is to be made of coarse new cereal parched with fire. Further instructions specify that not only the cereal offering but also indeed all offerings shall be seasoned with what is called the "salt of the covenant of your God" (2:13; see also Num 18:19). The torah of the cereal offering (Lev 6:14-18; MT, LXX 6:7-11) adds the supplementary directive that the dough of the baked cereal offering must be unleavened (6:17; MT, LXX 6:10). Given these directives for the selection and preparation of the sacrificial substances, the cereal offering clearly belongs to the domain of food.

A further characteristic of the actual ritual of the cereal offering is its brevity. The procedure at the sanctuary consists only of the apportionment, that is, the burning of a portion of the substances, which is further emphasized through the addition of all of the frankincense; the apportionment concludes with the subsequent consumption of the rest of the cereal offering by the priest. Both aspects indicate that the cereal offering is clearly understood as food and that the burning rite on the altar is important.

These aspects are made explicit by the addition of various interpretive terms in the ritual instructions. First, its quality as an offering of food is conveyed through the term "offering [*qorbān*] for YHWH" (Lev 2:1, 4, 7, 12), which also expresses the dynamic movement of the sacrificial process through sacred space. It is interesting to note that the cereal offering is thus considered a sacrifice despite the fact that there is no victim. Second, the metamorphosis and transport through the burning rite and its acceptance by God are captured by the terms "an offering by fire, a pleasing odor for YHWH" (2:2, 9, 12, 16; 6:15 [MT, LXX 6:8]). Third, the additional interpretive term "memorial portion" (Hebrew *'azkārâ*) occurs only in the context of the cereal offering (2:2; 6:15 [MT, LXX 6:8]; see also 5:12); it can be understood as a reference to God's promise given in the Altar Law to remember the offerer (see above, p. 33).

Also notable, fourth, is the absence of any mention of atonement in the context of this type of sacrifice. The reason might be that the cereal offering is primarily associated with joy and festivity; this is indicated through the mandatory addition of oil, which is most likely olive oil.[134]

The Septuagint renders *minḥâ*, the Hebrew technical term for the cereal offering, in most cases as *thysia* while employing five different terms less frequently. The Greek term *thysia* is usually translated as "sacrifice"; there is a consensus, however, that this term specifically denotes the ritual activity of slaughter. The use of *thysia* in reference to a sacrifice from vegetal substances reveals that this common opinion needs revision. According to the cosmology of the Hebrew Bible, vegetal substances cannot be slaughtered, and we have seen that the ritual of the cereal offering does not feature anything that resembles such an activity.[135] Why then does the Septuagint translate *minḥâ* as *thysia*? The answer requires a reevaluation of the meaning of this Greek term. Royden K. Yerkes suggests that, originally, this Greek term referred not to slaughter but to fumigation.[136] When positing the broader meaning of *thysia* as "sacrifice," referring to the entire ritual activity of a cultic sacrifice, then both slaughter and the burning rite are comprised. Only this broader meaning of the term *thysia* explains why it was considered appropriate to translate Hebrew *minḥâ*.

The Sacrifice of Well-Being

The remainder of the sacrificial instructions in Leviticus 4–7 features three other types of sacrifice, all of which are animal sacrifices. Due to the limited space of this study, the following description discusses only characteristic features extensively.

The Hebrew term for the sacrifice of well-being is *zebâḥ šělāmîm*. Contrary to the other four types of sacrifice in the priestly cult system, this is a combined term, and partially due to this, the English translation is much disputed. The phrase has been translated as "sacrifice of peace offering,"[137] "sacrifice of peace-offerings,"[138] "peace offering,"[139] "sacrifice of well-being,"[140] "well-being offering,"[141] or "fellowship offering."[142] The ritual of the sacrifice of well-being is featured in Leviticus 3:1-17; additional information is contained in 7:11-34.

> If his offering is a sacrifice of well-being, if he offers an animal of the herd, whether male or female, he shall offer it without blemish before YHWH. And he shall lean his hand on the head of his offering and slaughter it at the entrance of the tent of meeting; and Aaron's sons, the priests, shall dash the blood against all sides of the altar. And he shall offer from the sacrifice of well-being an offering by fire to YHWH: the suet that covers the entrails and all the suet that is around the entrails; the two kidneys and the suet that is around them on the sinews, and the caudate lobe of the liver, which he shall remove with the kidneys. And Aaron's sons shall burn these on the altar, with the burnt offering that is upon the wood on the fire; [this is] an offering by fire of pleasing odor to YHWH.

Other animals appropriate for a sacrifice of well-being are those of the flock, namely sheep (Lev 3:6-11) or goats (3:12-17); birds are not permitted. The animal is to be slaughtered in the outer areas of the court or alternatively, according to Leviticus 17:3, at the home of the offerer. The suet, the most valuable part of the animal, and other inner organs are to be burned on the altar.[143] The ritual resembles that of the burnt offering with the exception that most of the sacrificial meat is for the offerer and his family or clan who usually consume it at a celebration; some of the meat is for the officiating priests. For example, according to the story about the annual pilgrimage of Elkanah and his family (1 Sam 1), portions of the sacrifice were shared with all family members. The cheerful and merry atmosphere of such an event is the reason why the priest of the local sanctuary assumed that Hannah, Elkanah's childless wife, might be drunk (vv. 13-14).[144]

The ritual of this sacrifice thus continues beyond the process at the sanctuary.[145] These characteristic aspects are specified and further elaborated on in the torah of the sacrifice of well-being (Lev 7:11-34). It distinguishes different occasions for this sacrifice, "for thanksgiving" (7:12), "a votive offering," or "a freewill offering" (7:16), each of which should be accompanied by unleavened cakes, unleavened wafers, cakes, and oil (see also Num 6:17; 15:8-10). Moreover, it stipulates that the meat of this sacrifice must be consumed within one (Lev 7:15) or two days (7:16-18). These regulations also prohibit the eating of suet and blood (3:17; 7:23-25). Contrary to modern dietary customs, suet was considered the choice part of the animal in antiquity; in other contexts, the Hebrew term for suet can also mean "best of" (Num 18:12, 29-32; Ps 147:14). For this reason, the suet of the sacrificial animal is reserved for God alone.

The burning rite is emphasized in a variety of ways: More than half of the text of the ritual is dedicated to the exact parts of the sacrificial animal that are to be burned, and the burning itself. This ritual activity is again accompanied by interpretive comments. Peculiar is the fact that the term "offering by fire" (*'iššeh*) occurs twice,

once to introduce the list of the sacrificial material to be burnt, and once to conclude the burning
rite. The last interpretive comment on the ritual is
even further extended: "[this is] food, an offering
by fire for a pleasing odor; all suet is for YHWH"
(Lev 3:16). In connection with the supplementary
instructions of the torah of the well-being sacrifice, this sacrifice clearly emerges as a primary
source of food for God and humans.

However, the sacrifice of well-being is rarely
ever connected with atonement since its consumption typically takes place in the context of a cheerful celebration. It is thus once more questionable
whether the hand-leaning gesture and atonement
can be generally correlated.

The Sin Offering

The predominantly joyous atmosphere of the
cereal offering and of the sacrifice of well-being
changes as we study the remaining two types of
sacrifice. Their descriptions both start with specific
sins that have been committed by the offerer and
are structured by who committed them. The sacrifices, then, effect atonement: "They expiate for
sin: the violation of prohibitive commandments or
the violation of sanctums."[146]

The first of these two expiatory sacrifices is
the sin offering, ḥaṭṭā't in Hebrew.[147] Its ritual is
featured in Leviticus 4:1–5:13; supplementary
instructions are found in the torah of the sin offering (6:24-30; MT, LXX 6:17-23). The first ritual is
for a priest who sinned; he is to offer a bull (4:1-
12). The second ritual is as follows (4:13-21):

If the whole community of Israel sins unintentionally and the matter escapes the notice of the assembly so that they violate any of the commands of Yhwh, even though the community is unaware of the matter, they are guilty. When they become aware of the sin they committed, the assembly must bring a bull of the herd as a sin offering and bring it before the Tent of Meeting. The elders of the community shall lean their hands on the bull's head before Yhwh, and the bull shall be slaughtered before Yhwh. Then the anointed priest shall take some of the bull's blood into the Tent of Meeting. And the priest shall dip his finger in the blood and sprinkle it before Yhwh seven times in front of the curtain. He shall put some of the blood on the horns of the altar that is before Yhwh in the Tent of Meeting, and shall pour out the rest of the blood at the base of the altar of burnt offering at the entrance to the Tent of Meeting. He shall remove all the suet from it and burn it on the altar, and do with this bull just as he did with the bull for the sin offering. Thus the priest will make atonement for them, and they will be forgiven. Then he shall take the bull outside the camp and burn it as he burned the first bull. This is the sin offering for the community.

The third ritual specifies the sin offering of a leader of the community; this person must offer a male goat (Lev 4:22-26). The fourth describes the sin offering of an individual; this person must sacrifice a female goat (4:27-31) or a female sheep (4:32-35). Certain similarities between these rituals and previous ones are explicitly mentioned: the ritual of the sin offering of the community references the sin offering of the priest (4:20-21), and the sin offering of the common person references the well-being sacrifice (4:31). Both references are directed at the lengthy list of suet and organs that are to be removed from the sacrificial animal in order to be burned on the altar. These activities are thus comparable.

A characteristic difference, however, is the elaborate blood application rite. All animal sacrifices feature the activity of pouring out sacrificial blood at the base of the altar of burnt offering. The ritual of the sin offering, however, is the only one that inserts a blood application rite beforehand. The places and locations where the priest is to daub or sprinkle the blood differ: in front of the curtain of the sanctuary and on the horns of the golden altar of incense (Lev 4:6-7, 17-18), or on the horns of the altar of burnt offering (4:25, 30, 34; see also 16:18-19). Once per year, on the Day of Atonement, the high priest shall enter even the Holy of Holies and "shall take some of the blood of the bull, and sprinkle it with his finger on the front of the Mercy Seat, and before the Mercy Seat he shall sprinkle the blood with his finger seven times" (16:14). Thus, the blood of the sin offering is always applied to objects or appurtenances of the sanctuary.

A second characteristic difference is the removal of the remainder of the sacrificial animal at the end of the ritual. This remainder is either to be burned outside the camp (Lev 4:11-12, 21); the Hebrew verb employed here is *śrp,* which is different from *qtr* (*hiph'il*), which denotes only the burning on the altar. Or the priest is to eat the remainder. Pertinent regulations are found in the torah of the sin offering (Lev 6:24-30; MT, LXX Lev 6:17-23).

A third and somewhat intricate characteristic is the interpretive comments. An expiatory sacrifice, the sin offering features recurring formulas such as: "The priest will make atonement [Hebrew *kipper*] for him/them, and he/they will be forgiven." Atonement thus leads to the elimination of sins. Is it possible to further specify which ritual activity of the sin offering has such an atoning effect? Possibly in light of the rabbinic motto: "There is no atonement except through blood" (*Babylonian Talmud*, tractate *Yoma* 5a), blood rites are often considered to be the key to atonement. And indeed, the ritual of the Day of Atonement immediately connects the blood application rites in the Holy of Holies (Lev 16:14-15) with the interpretive comment: "Thus he [the priest] shall make atonement [Hebrew *kipper*] for the sanctuary, because of the impurities of the people of Israel, and because of their transgressions, all their sins" (16:16). To be noted, however, is that in the ritual of the sin offering in Leviticus 4:1–5:13, the interpretive comment about atonement and forgiveness (4:20, 26, 31, 35; 5:10, 13) *always* occurs immediately after the burning rite on the altar of burnt offering, which in turn is preceded by the blood rite. We may thus conclude that both the blood application rite *and* the burning rite effect atonement. The fact that the burning rite contributes to atonement is corroborated by a later appendix to the ritual (Lev 5:11-13). It allows poor people who cannot afford the purchase of more expensive sacrificial materials to offer a tenth of an *ephah* of fine flour instead. In this case, atonement is not effected by blood rites but only by the burning rite on the altar.

An important question regarding the blood application rites is: How and where is atonement accomplished? The description of the Day of Atonement evinces the understanding that sacrificial blood does not eliminate the guilt borne by humans but purges those objects and appurtenances to which it is actually applied. That is, it is effective upon physical contact. This interpretation comprises various aspects. First, the sanctuary itself is polluted by human sin and impurity (Lev 15:31; 16:16). Second, sacrificial blood, as the principal substance of life (17:11), is an effective cultic cleansing agent. This specific impersonal function is generally called "expiation": atonement is accomplished through the purgation of sin.[148] And third, all of this has to do with sacredness. According to supplementary directives in the torah of the sin offering (Lev 6:24-30; MT, LXX 6:17-23), the animal offered as a sin offering is "most holy." Therefore, accidental physical contact with the blood (and meat) of the sacrificial animal transmits its sacredness to an object (6:20; MT, LXX 6:27). The intentional physical contact during the ritual blood application performed by the priest likewise transmits this sacredness. Atonement (Hebrew root *kpr*) through blood application rites can thus be considered as a process of (re)consecration of sanctuary objects.[149]

The interpretive comments indicate that the elaborate blood application rites are the most

characteristic activity in the ritual of the sin offering. What about the burning rite on the altar? It
is to be noted, first, that those interpretive comments, which were always associated with the
burning rite in the ritual descriptions of burnt
offering, cereal offering, and well-being sacrifice,
occur less often in the ritual of the sin offering. On
the one hand, the formula "for a pleasing odor for
YHWH" occurs just once in the entire sin offering
ritual in Leviticus 4:1–5:13. The term "offering by
fire," on the other hand, occurs in a peculiarly different fashion: "He [the priest] shall remove all the
suet, just as the suet is removed from the lamb of
the well-being sacrifice, and the priest shall burn
it on the altar *upon the offerings by fire* of YHWH"
(Lev 4:35; see also 5:12). This unusual instruction
can be explained by studying other texts that deal
with a combination of different types of sacrifice
and allow further insights into the complexity of
ancient ritual processes. On the Day of Atonement,
for example, the high priest offers sin offerings
first (Lev 16:11, 15) and then applies their blood
(16:15-16, 18-19). Afterward he offers his burnt
offering and the burnt offering of the people "to
make atonement for himself and for the people"
(16:24); we know now that the burnt offering is
offered as an "offering by fire" and "for the pleasing odor for YHWH" (1:9; see above, pp. 66–68).
The instruction of the Day of Atonement continues: "He shall also burn the suet of the sin offering on the altar" (16:25). From this information,
we can conclude that the ritual of the sin offering
was interrupted after the blood application rite. Its
suet was not burned right away but *after* the burnt

offering has been burnt. If the suet of the sin offering is then placed on the altar, then the description
in Leviticus 4:35 is indeed correct: it is burned on
the altar upon the offerings by fire of YHWH. This
circumstance explains why interpretive comments
are less frequently attached to the burning rite of
the sin offering.

For this reason, the priestly texts do classify the
sin offering as an "offering [*qorbān*] for YHWH."
This interpretive term referencing the sacrificial
portion for God occurs repeatedly in the ritual of
the sin offering (Lev 4:23, 28, 32; 5:11). This means
that while the blood application rite is the most
characteristic ritual component of the sin offering,
the burning rite is also important. As we have just
seen in the ritual of the sin offering, the burning
rite of the sin offering also effects atonement.

The Guilt Offering

The ritual of the second of the expiatory sacrifices,
the guilt offering, is featured in Leviticus 7:1-6.
The Hebrew term for this type of sacrifice is *'āšām*.
In the Hebrew Bible, this sacrifice is the one mentioned the least frequently.

> This is the torah of the guilt offering; it is most
> holy. The guilt offering shall be slaughtered in
> the place where the burnt offering is slaughtered,
> and its blood shall be dashed against all sides of
> the altar. All of its suet shall be offered: the broad
> tail and the suet that covers the inner entrails,
> the two kidneys and the suet around them on the
> sinews, and the caudate lobe of the liver, which
> he shall remove with the kidneys. The priest shall

burn them on the altar; [this is] an offering by fire for YHWH. It is a guilt offering. Any male in a priest's family may eat of it; it must be eaten in a holy place; it is most holy.

Additional information about the occasions when the guilt offering must be presented is featured in Leviticus 5:14–6:7 (MT, LXX 5:14-26). A ram must be offered upon sacrilege, that is, offenses against sacred property, or in cases of intentional sins. In addition, "He [the offerer] shall make restitution for what he has failed to do in regard to the holy things and add one-fifth of the value to it and give it all to the priest, who will make atonement for him with the ram as a guilt offering, and he will be forgiven" (Lev 5:16). The requirement of combining a sacrifice and monetary payment is unique in the priestly sacrificial system.

The ritual of the guilt offering resembles that of the well-being sacrifice; however, no meat may be eaten by the offerer. In the regulations on purification from infectious skin diseases, the blood of a guilt offering is applied to the person to be cleansed (Lev 14:14, 25) in order to make atonement.

Alternative Ritual Means to Atonement

We have now studied the five types of sacrifice that form the priestly cult. As the most detailed and comprehensive instructions, the texts in Leviticus 1–7 are a good point of departure to approach the multifaceted reality of sacrifice in the Hebrew Bible. Further texts dating from different periods and belonging to other text genres would yield yet further aspects and provide interesting insights into the developments of the cult. Due to the limited scope of this study, focused as it is on the central parameters of the sacrificial cult, only few of these texts could be taken into consideration.

For ancient Israel and Judah, sacrifices were tokens for encountering God. Such encounter could happen under very different circumstances: in situations of joy and happiness or in situations of distress, suffering, and sin. Sacrifices were means that corresponded to all of these circumstances. They helped to establish ritualized settings of pleasant celebrations, but they also provided atonement in order to achieve forgiveness of sins.

Elimination Rituals

Sacrifices were, however, not the only means of atonement. Ancient Israel and Judah also knew elimination rituals that, compared to sacrifices, had very different inner logics.

The best-known elimination ritual in the Hebrew Bible is that of the scapegoat: On the Day of Atonement, the high priest transmits Israel's sin and impurity, perceived in a quasi-material fashion, onto a live goat. This animal is dispatched into the wilderness to dispose of the miasma (Lev 16:10, 20-22). Structurally similar processes can be found in the ritual for purification of skin disease (Lev 14:4-7) and the atonement ritual for unsolved murder (Deut 21:1-9).

Two aspects are important for this study: First, elimination rituals never count as sacrifices in the

Hebrew Bible. While sacrificial rituals are characterized by a gradual movement toward the sanctuary (see above, p. 71), the dynamics of elimination rituals are in each case directed away from the human habitat and toward uncultivated territory.[150] In spite of such opposite dynamics, however, sacrifices and elimination rituals share the purpose of effecting atonement since they eradicate evil. The second important aspect is the observation that the bird or goat carrying the miasma away is not killed. They only "escape" (hence the name "scapegoat"). In elimination rituals, therefore, atonement can be obtained without the killing of an animal.

The Metaphorical Use of Sacrificial Terminology

In the history of ancient Israel and Judah, the centralization of the temple cult greatly limited the possibility for common people to participate in worship at the sanctuary in Jerusalem. This development reduced their attendance at sacrificial rituals to occasional pilgrimages. Given this situation, people did not abandon the concept of sacrifice but started to employ it as a metaphor or example. They drew on familiar technical terms or key concepts from priestly discourses on the sacrificial cult. Imported into other domains of daily life or even into the secular realm, this terminology opened new dimensions of articulating concerns ranging from religious practice and ethics to warfare. Thus, the following phrase came to capture an appropriate pious attitude: "The sacrifices [*zibḥê*] of God are a broken spirit" (Ps 51:17 MT, LXX

Psalm 51:19). The sacrifices and the recommended attitude share several common aspects: both are directed to God, both are genuine human expressions of worship, and God accepts either one. Also in the following prayer, the specific usage of the sacrificial terminology suggests that it is actually a cultic metaphor: "Accept the free-will offerings [*nidbôt*] of my mouth, O Yᴴᵂᴴ, and teach me your ordinances" (Ps 119:108).[151]

However, technical terms from the sacrificial cult have also been referred to humans. In a vision of the future salvation of Israel and the restoration of Jerusalem, the prophet Isaiah describes people from all nations as they come to glorify God. Because of their worship, they are then compared to sacrifices: "They will bring all your kindred from all the nations as an offering [*minḥâ*] for Yᴴᵂᴴ, on horses and in chariots . . . to my holy mountain Jerusalem, says Yᴴᵂᴴ, just as the Israelites bring a cereal offering in a clean vessel to the house of Yᴴᵂᴴ" (Isa 66:20). This terminology specifically references the dynamics that underlie every sacrificial ritual as it gradually moves toward the center of holiness at the sanctuary (see above, p. 71).

Cultic metaphors were also employed by the Judean community in Qumran. Some of their scrolls (also called "Dead Sea Scrolls") attest that they were used to label righteous behavior. In the *Rule of the Community* (1QS), for instance, a community council composed of twelve men and three priests is expected to live in perfect obedience to the laws of the Torah. When this happens, "[it will be] the most holy dwelling for Aaron with eternal knowledge of the covenant of justice in order to offer a pleasing odor [Hebrew *rêaḥ-nîḥôaḥ*]. . . . And these will be accepted in order to atone [Hebrew *kipper*] for the land . . . and there will be no iniquity" (1 QS 8:8-10).

This text contains a variety of cultic terms and images. First, the quality of the community council as "most holy" references not only the special sacredness of objects and appurtenances in the sanctuary but also that of its second chamber, called "the Holy of Holies." The "pleasing odor" refers to a key feature of the sacrificial cult, conveying that God accepts what humans offer. The idea that this brings about atonement for the land and purges it from iniquity is reminiscent of blood application rites on the Day of Atonement, which purge sin and defilement from the sanctuary. Hence in its *Rule of the Community*, the Qumran community does not dwell on any details of sacrificial rituals; it employs instead key notions of the spectrum of interpretive terms found in the sacrificial laws of Leviticus 1-7.

Finally, however, prophetic texts feature especially the Hebrew root *zbḥ* in its meaning "to slaughter" as a metaphor for the defeat of hostile armies. In Isaiah 34:6-7, for example, violent images show YHWH as a warrior wielding a sword against Edom in order to restore Zion. Some terminology is taken from sacrificial rituals: "For a sacrifice [Hebrew *zebaḥ*] for YHWH is in Bozrah and a great slaughter in Edom" (34:6). Such visions of vengeance might be rooted in historical conflicts between ancient Israel and the Edomites, who probably participated in the destruction of

Jerusalem.[152] In a similar fashion, Jeremiah 46:10-12 envisions how God will kill many on "a day of retribution"; indeed, God "holds a sacrifice [Hebrew *zebaḥ*] in the land of the north by the river Euphrates" (46:10). It is only natural that ancient nomadic cultures, very familiar with the act of animal slaughter, employed this image in visions of warfare.

Yet considering the frequent modern usage of the term *sacrifice* that largely connotes loss and misfortune, it is important to mention that, in the Hebrew Bible, metaphors connoting death and destruction are limited to the Hebrew root *zbḥ* and that they are rare. They barely match the abundance and import of the modern usage of *sacrifice*. In biblical narratives, for example, neither Abram's willingness to exchange his home in Haran for an uncertain future (Gen 12) nor David's readiness to stay at the royal court despite Saul's repeated assaults on his life (1 Sam 18:10-11) are ever articulated in sacrificial terminology.

Summary: The Meaning of Sacrifice in the Hebrew Bible

Sacrifice in the Bible is a multivalent category. Its origins in the biblical world were complex rituals that common people were familiar with since they actually carried them out or watched them more or less frequently. Such rituals could comprise many distinct elements. Common to all types of sacrifice (including the cereal offering) is selecting the appropriate material for a particular type of sacrifice, bringing it to the sanctuary, and arranging some or all of it on the main altar for the burning rite. Specific to animal sacrifices is leaning one's hand on the animal's head, slaughtering it, applying its blood at special locations, and then pouring the remainder out at the base of the altar, skinning the animal, cutting it apart, removing certain parts to be burned, and in some cases consuming other parts. The cereal offering, however, features special attention to the proper preparation of the vegetal material that, at the sanctuary, is partially burned and partially consumed by the priests.

Scholars interpreting such rituals have tended to focus on just one or some of these ritual elements and given priority to animal ("bloody") sacrifices. Only recently have some scholars, adopting a polythetic approach, regarded the entire ritual sequence and included vegetal sacrifices in their theorizing. Attention to selected ritual elements could, of course, create multiple interpretive associations. "It would be preferable to see sacrifice as a *multivalent entity*. Various explanations of its function could coexist, and what a given writer enunciates is also affected by the literary needs and genre of the writer in question," recommends Gary A. Anderson.[153] This explains the large number of different answers to the question of what "the meaning" of sacrifice is. In light of its ritual complexity, it is more appropriate to ask: What are the meanings of sacrificial rituals or of the sacrifices?

The main characteristics and aspects of sacrifices in the priestly system of the Hebrew Bible that I have studied above can be summarized further as follows:

1. A fundamental precondition for the sacrificial cult is an essential *separation* between the earthly and the heavenly domain (see above, p. 69). Sacrifices help to bridge this separation, allowing humans to *approach the sacred location* of God's presence. This dynamic movement is expressed by the comprehensive Hebrew term for sacrifice, *qorbān*. Every type of sacrifice in the priestly system is called *qorbān* (Lev 1:2; 7:38). Translated as "offering," this term also conveys that sacrifices can be understood as *tokens of homage* to God (see above, p. 69).

2. All five types of sacrifice in the priestly system have *specific characteristics*: The burnt offering is *entirely given* to God; the cereal offering is prepared from *vegetal substances*; a pleasant "side effect" of the well-being sacrifice is a *meal* (and celebration) for the offerer; the sin offering *expiates* the sanctuary *from defilement* due to involuntary human offenses; the guilt offering atones also for intentional sins by *monetary compensation*.

3. The act of *killing* naturally occurs only in animal sacrifices but *not* in all types of sacrifice. The priestly texts lack any indication that this ritual element had special significance, as several theories of sacrifice postulate (see above pp. 17, 18, 19, 20). This means that *ritualized killing is not the purpose of cultic sacrifices* in the Hebrew Bible, and killing alone does not qualify a given set of activities as a sacrifice (see above, p. 28).

4. Likewise, the approach of choosing the *blood application rite* as *interpretive key* to the *entire* phenomenon of sacrifice in the Hebrew Bible (see above, pp. 15, 22–23) is *problematic*. According to the laws in Leviticus 1–7, only one type of sacrifice, the sin offering, regularly features such an activity. Its blood application rites effect *purification* and *consecration* upon physical contact. They are a key element in expiatory sacrifices. According to Leviticus 17:11, sacrificial blood *represents the life of the animal* (see above, p. 86). No biblical text warrants the interpretation that existential substitution occurs in sacrificial rituals of the Hebrew Bible.

5. It is important to take *all sacrificial substances* into consideration. The *cereal offering*, prepared from vegetal materials, oil, and frankincense, also deserves attention in modern theorizing on sacrifice. Its ritual displays the importance of apportionment, and thus of the burning rite. It is important for modern theorizing that the priestly cult system knows of a type of sacrifice that "functions" *without any victim* (see above, p. 78).

6. Sacrificial substances are *foodstuff*; their preparation is analogous to that of *meals*. As such, ritual sacrifices aim at *honoring God* and establishing a lasting *relationship* between humans and God (see above, p. 75).

7. Sacrificial rituals can effect *atonement*. Both *blood application rites and the burning rite* contribute in their specific fashion to

atonement: the former consecrates through the animal's life (*expiation*), and the latter appeases through the "pleasing odor for YHWH" (*propitiation*).

8. The *burning rite* on the main altar is the *only* ritual element that is part of *all five types of sacrifice* of the priestly system in Leviticus 1–7. Through the altar fire, material offerings are sublimated into an ethereal quality ("offering by fire") and ascend to the heavenly sphere, where they are accepted by God (see above, p. 67).

9. *Interpretive terms* such as "to atone," "to forgive," "to make acceptable," "offering by fire," "pleasing odor," and "offering for YHWH" provide important insights into how sacrifices "function" and should be taken into consideration for modern theorizing on sacrifice.

10. Since all rituals that feature this burning rite are called an "offering for YHWH," this rite can be interpreted as the *constitutive element of sacrifice*. This means: in the priestly cult system, all ritual sequences that feature the burning of materials on the altar of burnt offering are considered as sacrifices.

This final aspect is important for the discussion of the nature of sacrifices. If the burning rite is recognized as the constitutive element of sacrifices, then a clear distinction can be drawn between other activities such as elimination rituals or (random) acts of killing, even if these are said to effect atonement.

Further ramifications pertain to terminology. According to common parlance, the word *offering* is the broader term that means more generally "gift/oblation," while *sacrifice* is any such offering that involves an act of killing. Such an understanding needs to be revised.[154] It presupposes a terminological distinction that can be traced to Thomas Aquinas (1225–74 C.E.) but does not exist anywhere in biblical vocabulary.[155] In the Hebrew Bible, in fact, no comprehensive term exists that applies exclusively to animal sacrifices. The term "offering for YHWH" is applied to rituals regardless of whether they are animal or cereal sacrifices. The modern perception and interpretation of sacrificial rituals in the Hebrew Bible should be adjusted to reflect these parameters. Then it is clear that the sacrificial tradition of Judaism is not bent on violence or death. For that matter, even our modern term *sacrifice* does not specifically denote killing in sequences of ritual activity.[156] Derived from the Latin *sacrificium*, the term means "to make sacred" or "to dedicate" and therefore designates the aspect of consecration through giving to God.

The understanding that substances offered by humans are sublimated into "offerings by fire" and accepted by God does, of course, presuppose a worldview informed by theology or religion. It necessarily accepts the symbolic dimension of ritual sacrifices and, following the interpretive terminology of the priestly texts, assumes that their function and value can be described in relation to this framework. While many contemporary approaches committed to ritual theory display reluctance toward any symbolic understanding of sacrifices or larger interpretive framework (see above, p. 24), Gerald A. Klingbeil acknowledges their "*symbolic dimension*, which suggests that in rituals expression and communication are achieved by means of symbolic action."[157]

When we acknowledge a symbolic interpretive framework, then we can explain the sacrifices in Leviticus 1–7 as offerings to God. From this perspective, it is possible to account for the order of the five types of sacrifice featured there. The burnt offering is listed first since God is its only recipient. The cereal offering is second as it is shared between God, who receives a handful of the vegetal substance, and the priest, who receives the remainder. The well-being offering is third as it has three recipients: God, the priest, and the offerer. The expiatory sacrifices are listed after these three; they form their own category. Among these, the sin offering is first as it must be offered in case of unintentional sin; the guilt offering is second because it is for graver offenses and intentional sins.

These reflections, if seen in correlation with the issues mentioned in the introductory chapter of this study, address three of the popular concerns regarding sacrifice. One concern was the perception that sacrifice and atonement were connected to death. Our study of sacrifice and atonement in the Hebrew Bible, however, has demonstrated that the act of slaughter is not inherently but is, rather, coincidentally connected to sacrifice. Sacrifice is possible without killing and without victim, and atonement is partially based on the force of life. A second concern was violence in sacrifice. Yet our study of sacrifice revealed that violence, namely animal slaughter, is limited to the introductory stage of the ritual. Most of the sacrificial ritual is dedicated to apportionment and the burning rite. The cereal offering, of course, has no ritual activity that could possibly be considered as violent given the cosmology of the Hebrew Bible. And third, concepts of substitution that assume the innocent suffers vicariously for a guilty party do not emerge from the sacrificial cult of the Hebrew Bible.

2

The Sacrifice of Jesus

Understanding Christological Atonement Metaphors

They are now justified freely by his grace
through the redemption in Christ Jesus,
whom God put forth as a place of atonement
through faith in his blood.

ROMANS 3:25

In this chapter, I investigate how the tradition of sacrificial rituals of ancient Israel and Judah that was outlined in the previous chapter was applied by early Christians to envision and proclaim the salvation brought by Jesus Christ. Primarily the following terms were used as metaphors: the nouns "sacrifice/offering," "blood," "lamb," and "(place of) atonement;" the verbs "to offer" and "to atone;" and the interpretive comments "for a pleasing odor" and "acceptable." Some of these words and phrases originated in the creative process of early Christians to interpret and communicate the entire mission of Jesus, including his shocking death. Yet early Christians were guided in their interpretive endeavor by the proposals of Jesus to understand his mission in cultic terms. Nevertheless, today these metaphors are often rejected due to a perception of negative or violent connotations. I will show, however, that sacrificial metaphors in christological contexts do not exclusively express violence or vicarious death, but connote holiness and acceptance. Early Christian Christology thus appears in a very different light.[158]

Jesus the Sacrifice

In our survey of the Hebrew Bible above, we encountered sacrifice usually within actual sacrificial rituals. Specifically designated sacrificial materials were offered on altars by persons who were usually priests or had special standing in front of God. Sacrificial terminology also occurred as metaphors, albeit not very often. In the writings of the New Testament, this situation is inversed. These texts feature only few references to actual sacrifices, while sacrificial metaphors are more frequent. For example, Jesus is never portrayed as offering an actual sacrifice at the temple of Jerusalem. He recommends that others offer sacrifices according to the Judean tradition (Matt 8:4 with reference to Lev 14:2-32), emphasizes that personal reconciliation with somebody has priority over sacrifice (Matt 5:23-24), or occasionally quotes prophetic words that convey a critical stance toward the sacrificial cult (Matt 9:13; 12:7; with quotes from Hos 6:6). Also, Paul makes some sporadic comments about pagan sacrifices, which he contrasts to the Eucharist (1 Cor 10:18, 20).

Overall, however, actual sacrifices are not mentioned frequently in the New Testament.

The term *sacrifice*, though, is frequently used as a metaphor in New Testament letters. The continuous confession of God's name and simple acts of sharing with others can be labeled "sacrifice [*thysia*]" (Heb 13:15-16). The usage of these metaphors for particular religious behavior is fully analogous to sacrificial metaphors in the Hebrew Bible (see above, pp. 91–92). More unusual is the way Paul employs such cultic vocabulary. He encourages members of the congregation in Rome to present their bodies "as a living sacrifice" (Rom 12:1) and later calls himself a minister of Christ Jesus who brings the "offering of the Gentiles" (15:16). Paul's statement in Philippians 2:17 is difficult to comprehend: "But even if I am being poured out like a libation over the sacrifice and service of your faith, I am glad and rejoice with all of you." It is likely that the apostle uses these cult metaphors with the intention of showing how his own mission is dovetailed with the life of the congregation.[159] In these various instances, Paul applies sacrificial terminology to people (including himself). The imagery conveys that they are ultimately engaged in God's mission.

Given the abundance of modern references to the sacrifice of Jesus, it is surprising that the New Testament Gospels never use the term *sacrifice* with reference to Jesus. (On the predication of Jesus as "lamb," see below.) In fact, the New Testament features only two writings in which Jesus is explicitly referred to in that way. To be sure, the sacrifice of Jesus is also alluded to in references to his blood, when he is called "(place of) atonement," and so on. Yet only in one passage, Ephesians 5:2, and several times in the Letter to the Hebrews is Jesus indeed called a "sacrifice."[160] As a separate section will be dedicated to the Letter to the Hebrews, I will, for the moment, only deal with the Letter to the Ephesians. It features the following sentences: "Therefore be imitators of God, as beloved children. And walk in love, just as Christ loved us, too, and gave himself for us as an *offering and sacrifice for God as a pleasing odor*" (Eph 5:1-2). The terminology that is derived from the Judean sacrificial cult (italicized text) employs two different Greek nouns for "sacrifice," *prosphora* and *thysia*. Among these, the latter could, in the sacrificial regulations of the Hebrew Bible, refer to the cereal offering (Lev 2; see above, p. 78). The former is only attested once in the Septuagint, namely in Psalm 40:6 (MT 39:7) where it translates the term *minḥâ* ("cereal offering"). It is thus doubtful that, following the traditional interpretation, these sacrificial terms could refer exclusively to the death of Jesus. The addition of the interpretive comment, Greek *osmē euōdias*, which usually accompanies the burning rite, bears this out: this metaphor references the effect of ritual sacrifices. Moreover, the passage in Ephesians 5:1-2 is the center of gravity of a larger paraenetic section that comprises Ephesians 4:1–6:9. It contains a variety of practical instructions on proper behavior (for example, patience, 4:2; avoiding anger, 4:26; compassion and forgiveness, 4:32). The question arises as to how these instructions might relate to the "sacrifice" of Jesus. It is indeed difficult to imagine that the death on the cross could be referenced as the paradigm for such practical conduct.

What then does the sacrificial terminology in Ephesians 5:2 mean? Based on my reevaluation of the meaning of sacrifice in the Hebrew Bible, this metaphor cannot focus exclusively on Christ's death on the cross or its violence. It rather conveys that his entire mission and life were of a special quality and, as a genuine expression of worship, accepted by God. Christ's righteous behavior as well as his teachings and miraculous signs, then, made God's love manifest as the center of salvation. These actions were recommended to the members of the congregation in Ephesus as the example that they were to follow in their own behavior. With this meaning, the term *sacrifice* has surprisingly positive connotations—at least compared to its modern understanding that is bent on loss, misfortune, and destruction.

In short: The sacrificial metaphors in Ephesians 5:2 suggest that the mission of Jesus was acceptable for God. They encourage the Christian congregation to listen carefully to the gospel story and act according to Christ's example.

Now we shall examine other sacrificial metaphors in the New Testament; we will see that they derive from different sacrificial activities and images.

The Blood of Jesus

The term *sacrifice* is not the only expression that represents sacrificial imagery in the New Testament. References to the blood of Jesus may also be derived from sacrificial rituals since blood application rites were important ritual activities, as we have seen (see above, p. 84).[161] Thus, phrases like "sprinkled with the blood of Jesus" (1 Pet 1:2; see also Rom 3:25; Eph 2:13) reflect traditional Judean sacrificial categories of atonement. Do these passages convey that Jesus died a vicarious death for humans, which means that Jesus died instead of us?

The context of some of these references about the blood of Jesus explicitly describes the effect. For instance, 1 John 1:7 states that "if we walk in the light, as he [God] is in the light, we have fellowship with one another, and the blood of Jesus his Son cleanses us from all sin." While the idea of walking in the light is similar to that of walking in love mentioned in Ephesians 5:2, the blood of Jesus is then said to purify humans. It achieves human holiness because sin, described as a general human predicament (1 John 1:10), is removed; it effects expiation. An analogous metaphor occurs in a vision of martyrs at the throne of God who "have washed their robes and made them white in the blood of the Lamb" (Rev 7:14). The idea that blood could render robes white is, of course, paradoxical and should not be taken literally. However, blood is once more understood as a cleansing agent.

The idea that sacrificial blood is a cultic cleansing agent is a well-documented feature of the ancient Israelite and Judean cult, as we have seen (see above, p. 86). Yet while the blood of sin offerings is always applied to sanctuary objects, where it effects purification and consecration

(Lev 4; 16), the New Testament passages assume that the blood of Jesus has been sprinkled upon humans. Are there Israelite or Judean traditions that account for such a usage? In fact, the Hebrew Bible narratives of the priestly ordination ceremonies and of the Mosaic covenant at Mount Sinai relate such blood application rites. In Exodus 29 and Leviticus 8, priests are consecrated by Moses, who first smears sacrificial blood on their ears, thumbs, and toes and then sprinkles it on them (Exod 29:20-21/Lev 8:23-24, 30). This peculiar combination of rites prepares the priests for their service at the sanctuary in front of the holy God of Israel. It corroborates the interpretation suggested above that blood application actually effects consecration and expiation. In a similar fashion and for a similar purpose, Moses sprinkles the blood of burnt offerings and sacrifices of well-being on the people of Israel at Mount Sinai (Exod 24:1-11). He calls this blood the "blood of the covenant" (v. 8). Then Moses and Israel's elders climb on the mountain, where they see God and have a celebration (vv. 10-11). Their appearing in front of God may be seen as a parallel to the service of the newly consecrated priests in front of God. Thus, Israel becomes God's priestly nation.

In line with the modus operandi of blood application rites in the Hebrew Bible, the conceptual idea behind the "blood of Jesus" has been determined as purification and consecration. This means that it does not first and foremost convey vicarious death. On the one hand, Christ's death makes his life available. On the other hand, while

Christ's death effects salvation for humans, the idea is not that Christ died instead of humans. As a consecrated and priestly community, then, Christians are invited to engage in daily worship.

In short: Early Christians used some cultic motifs in order to convey that Christ's death could save humans. However, the metaphor of his blood that is sprinkled on humans or that washed the robes of martyrs does not express vicarious death but, in accordance with traditional Israelite and Judean atonement concepts, the sacredness of Christ's *life*. This blood has the power of consecrating Christians so that they become holy. Like priests at the Judean sanctuary, they are invited to live their lives "in front of" God, namely as a form of continuous worship.

The Eucharistic Image of the "Blood of the Covenant"

Early Christianity adopted concepts of consecration derived from the traditional Judean sacrificial cult. According to the Hebrew Bible, such consecration occurs when physical contact is established between sacrificial blood and either sanctuary objects or humans. This leads to the corollary question: How can Christians claim that they have been in contact with the blood of Jesus? Would this not necessitate their presence at the cross of Jesus? If the blood of Jesus symbolizes his life and thus consecrates humans, how do humans partake of it?

These questions lead us to the Eucharist, or Last Supper, the central celebration of Christianity.[162]

According to the key New Testament texts (Matt 26:26-29; Mark 14:22-25; Luke 22:17-20; 1 Cor 11:23-26), Jesus instituted it before his death on the cross. While celebrating a Passover meal with his disciples, he took bread and a cup of wine, gave them to his disciples, and spoke the words of institution: "Take; this is my body" (Mark 14:22), and: "This is my blood of the covenant, which is poured out for many" (Mark 14:24), or: "This cup is the new covenant in my blood" (1 Cor 11:25). Of these words, only those spoken over the cup are derived from the sacrificial cult (the meaning of the eucharistic bread will be discussed below on pp. 127–28). Quoting from the Torah story about Israel's encounter with God at Mount Sinai, Jesus evoked scenes that were considered formative for ancient Israelite and Judean identity when he referenced the "blood of the covenant" (Exod 24:8).[163] Jesus instituted his covenant with wine, a traditional substitute for blood. Based on the analogy to the Mosaic covenant, this wine represented and communicated his life, but through the addition of the words "poured out" (Mark 14:24), also his impending death. According to the modus operandi of cultic application rites, physical contact with this new "blood of the covenant" effects forgiveness of sins (Matt 26:28) and thus expiates. Like the "blood of Jesus," this concept does not express his vicarious death for humans. Through the eucharistic wine, the Christian congregation becomes a holy community because its members are being consecrated. Jesus instituted an event with a powerful legacy that was easily recognized and understood by his contemporaries through the reference to the well-known Torah story of the Mosaic covenant.

This explanation of the words of institution spoken over the eucharistic cup implies that Jesus himself referenced the sacrificial cult when he made proposals as to how his disciples should interpret his mission and death. Given the gradually escalating conflict between him and the religious authorities of his time, he was likely to have anticipated his death when he approached Jerusalem. Using the sacrificial cult and atonement as an interpretive framework, Jesus referenced a familiar and high-profile institution of the very city in which he died one day later.

In short: The eucharistic wine, which represents the blood of Jesus, has cultic connotations. Derived from the Mosaic covenant at Mount Sinai, the new "blood of the covenant" has the power to consecrate those who drink of it so that their sins are forgiven. Thus, they become a holy and priestly community.

The Self-Sacrifice of Jesus according to the Letter to the Hebrews

The Letter to the Hebrews has its own characteristic Christology, in which the author postulates that the office Jesus holds is "better" than various representatives and institutions of the old covenant. For this purpose, Hebrews offers a detailed (albeit slightly modified) description of the tabernacle as backdrop of the cultic scenery (Heb 9:1-5) and of the sacrificial procedures on the Day of Atonement (9:6-10). Key in this overall exposition is the audacious combination of heterogeneous elements of the temple cult. First, the functions of priest and sacrifice are merged: Jesus appears as a high priest according to the order of Melchizedek (Heb 4:14–5:10), who at the same time offers himself "once for all" (Greek *ephapax*) as a sacrifice (7:27; 10:10, 12, 14). Second, the motif of sacrifice itself is fused with, and influenced by, that of blood; nowhere else in the New Testament are both of these terms used as abundantly with reference to Jesus as in Hebrews. Yet through their combination, the author of Hebrews ultimately transcends and reframes traditional sacrificial metaphors to fit the general christological program set out in Hebrews 2:14: salvation through Christ is accomplished through his death.

However, the traditional usage of sacrificial blood is initially affirmed, yet combined with, and ultimately influenced by, the notion of blood representing death: "According to the law, almost everything is purified with blood, and without the shedding of blood there is no forgiveness of sins" (Heb 9:22). Thus, Christ is said to have "entered into the sanctuary once for all, not with the blood of goats and calves, but with his own blood to obtain an eternal redemption" (Heb 9:12). Despite the parallel to the blood of animals, this is an allusion to Christ's death.[164] It appears as the necessary prerequisite for accessing the true, heavenly sanctuary where Christ henceforth sits at the right hand of God to advocate on behalf of humans.

In short: The Letter to the Hebrews creatively combines cultic parameters and envisions a better cult under the new covenant. According to its concepts, the blood of Christ, the high priest, consecrates, while his self-sacrifice that was made once for all times now focuses on his death as the precondition of accessing heaven. This concept literally opens the door to a new aspect of salvation, namely that of Christ's intercession on behalf of humans.

Jesus the (Place of) Atonement

Earlier I observed that, with the exception of the Letter to the Hebrews, Jesus is rarely ever called a "sacrifice" in the New Testament. Given the frequency of atonement terminology in the Hebrew Bible and the abundance of atonement theology in the modern Christian church, it is likewise interesting to note that atonement terminology is rarely employed in the New Testament. The Greek word for "to atone" or "to make atonement" is *hilaskomai*; in the Septuagint, it translates Hebrew *kipper*, which often occurs in sacrificial rituals of the Hebrew Bible (see above, p. 86). But in the New Testament, this word and its derivatives occur only four times with reference to Jesus.[165]

The verb *hilaskomai* occurs in Hebrews 2:17, where it is used to explain that Jesus became like humans "so that he might become merciful and a faithful high priest in his service to God, to make atonement for the sins of the people." It thus comprehensively captures Christ's priestly task according to the distinctive Christology of the Letter to the Hebrews. The subsequent lengthy descriptions of sacrificial rituals may, in fact, be considered as a detailed explanation of this office of making atonement.

Paul uses the Greek lexeme *hilaskomai* only once; indeed, he encounters it in a confession or hymn of the early Christian church.[166] Adopting much of this traditional text in his letter to the congregations in Rome, Paul articulates in "one of his most densely packed sentences"[167] that salvation in Christ is available although all humans have sinned: "They [the sinful humans] are now justified freely by his grace through the redemption in Christ Jesus, whom God put forth as a place of atonement through faith in his blood" (Rom 3:25).

This core passage for the understanding of justification through grace alone contains the Greek term *hilastērion*. There is an ongoing debate regarding its meaning. It is clear that, due to the accompanying term "blood," this passage evokes sacrificial images. What then is the correct translation and exact meaning of *hilastērion*? Many English Bible versions render this Greek term as "sacrifice of atonement,"[168] while others translate it as "propitiation"[169] or "expiation."[170] The translation "sacrifice of atonement," however, is doubtful since, on the one hand, such a term is entirely absent from the entire Hebrew Bible and, on the other hand, the Septuagint never employs the term *hilastērion* to translate any type of sacrifice. Instead, the Septuagint uses this term to refer to the golden cover of the Ark called the "Mercy Seat" (Hebrew *kappōret*; see above, p. 38), where sacrificial blood is applied in order to "atone" (Hebrew *kipper*). The other occurrence of the term *hilastērion* in the New Testament refers, in fact, to this sanctuary appurtenance (Heb 9:5). Christ would then be visualized as that part of the tabernacle associated with God's presence (see above, pp. 55–56). Yet the Septuagint, in Ezekiel's vision of the sanctuary, also uses *hilastērion* to designate a ledge of the altar of burnt offering (Ezek 43:14, 17, 20). The altar was the object of periodic blood application rites as well. Hence, it is recommendable to translate *hilastērion* more broadly as "atonement" or "place of atonement."[171]

I would like to mention that this aspect alone has surprising potential. In the first century C.E., sacrifices at the temple of Jerusalem were the means through which people expected atonement to be made. The temple was thus the center of encountering God. Of course, in the Hebrew Bible the use of the term atonement is also attested in noncultic texts, where it expresses mediation between human parties in case of controversy. But with regard to Jesus, it would not have occurred to many people to associate particularly his shameful death on the cross with atonement or God's presence. The claim that God could be encountered in Jesus was, therefore, unexpected or even blasphemous to most people back then. Moreover, it is typical of Paul's soteriology that he depicts God as being the agent of "putting forth" Jesus as the place of atonement. God is not to be propitiated by humans but is the one who offers atonement and thus actively proposes salvation for humanity.

The observation that the term *hilastērion* is combined with the term *haima* ("blood") evinces the idea of expiation through blood application rites. We have seen that specifically the blood of the sin offering is sprinkled toward the Mercy Seat or the altar of burnt offering. As the principal substance of life, this blood has the power of purging these objects from sins and impurities (see above, pp. 84–86). Already the older confessional hymn that Paul decided to integrate into one of his letters had employed the idea that salvation through Christ can be articulated in analogy to this cult paradigm.

Similar ideas are conveyed in the First Letter of John, where Jesus is portrayed as "the atonement for our sins, and not for ours only but also for the sins of the whole world" (2:2). Both here and in 1 John 4:10, the Greek term for "atonement" is *hilasmos*. Comparable to the English translation of Romans 3:25, this term is often rendered as "atoning sacrifice."[172] The translation customs of the Septuagint are less clear in this case. Greek *hilasmos* can translate the term "sin offering" (Hebrew *ḥaṭṭā't*; see Ezek 44:27; 45:19 or the apocryphal texts 1 Esd 9:20; 2 Macc 3:33; 12:45). It renders, however, also a variety of other terms (e.g., Hebrew *hakkippurîm*–"atonement," Lev 25:9; Num 5:8; see also Greek *exhilasmos* in the apocryphal texts Sir 16:11; 18:12, 20).[173] Thus, *hilasmos* has to do with forgiveness, but its precise meaning remains blurred. It is, therefore, recommendable to translate this term more generally as "atonement."[174]

In short: The Greek lexeme *hilaskomai*, the Septuagint translation of Hebrew *kipper*, is usually rendered in English as "to atone" or "to make atonement." The New Testament utilizes this lexeme only a few times with reference to Christ. The term then conveys salvation through Christ according to traditional Israelite and Judean concepts of expiation: his blood has the power of purging sins and impurities because it represents life. In addition, the motif of Christ being the "place of atonement" imagines him as the location of God's presence on earth and depicts God as the agent of human salvation.

Jesus the Lamb

In the opening chapter of the Fourth Gospel, John the Baptizer is depicted as he salutes Jesus at their first encounter as "the lamb [Greek *amnos*] of God that takes away the sin of the world" (John 1:29; see also v. 36). Thus, a prominent christological title was coined; its Latin form, *agnus dei*, was later integrated into early Christian liturgies.

The salutation of Jesus as "Lamb" presupposes the identification of a human being with an animal. There are not many biblical examples for such identification. The famous story of Abraham's sacrifice, also called the "Binding of Isaac" (Hebrew *'aqedat Yiṣḥāq*, Gen 22:1-19), knows of the equation of a child and a lamb, even though this is, rather, substitution.[175] Perhaps more to the point, the psalmist adopts the perspective of a sheep when praying: "The Lord is my shepherd, I shall not want" (Ps 23:1). This imagery draws on an animal species that is most familiar in nomadic cultures around the globe and epitomizes weakness, innocence, and purity. These attributes fit Jesus, who renounced any expression of violence and led a life free from sin. He may thus be seen in analogy to the council described in the Dead Sea scroll titled *Rule of the Community*. Through perfect torah obedience, which would establish innocence, this council was supposed to eliminate iniquities and "make atonement" for the land (1

QS 8:8-10; see above, p. 93). Such a concept opens up new possibilities to understand the image of the "Lamb of God": as a reference to Christ's righteousness and holiness, it implies that he has the power to "take away the sin of the world." These images show that not every concept of eliminating sin necessarily operates through death. In nomadic cultures, lambs have symbolic value by themselves.

There are, however, several other aspects to this predication of Jesus as well. A prominent text in the Hebrew Bible is the Song of the Suffering Servant in Isaiah 52:13—53:12. It depicts an innocent person who, despite being oppressed and mistreated (today we could probably also say: being bullied), "did not open his mouth; like a lamb that is led to the slaughter, and like a sheep that is silent before its shearers, so he did not open his mouth" (Isa 53:7). This song repeats time and again that the servant vicariously suffers and bears the sin of others (53:4-6, 11-12). It does, in the end, also describe the servant's death for the transgressions of others (v. 8). With these features, the passage defies the traditional interpretation of affliction in the Hebrew Bible, as Joseph Blenkinsopp explains: "Whatever the sad condition of the servant, . . . the speaker and no doubt many in the community at first accepted the *interpretatio communis*, amply illustrated in Psalms and Job, that his condition was the result of divine punishment for sin: he was stricken, smitten by God, and afflicted (53:4b)."[176]

Due to its unique profile, the Song of the Suffering Servant is the only Hebrew Bible text that conveys vicarious suffering and the surrender of somebody's life for another.[177] It must, however, be mentioned that it does not draw on any cultic background. The parallel to shearing in Isaiah 53:7 suggests that the lamb's slaughter is also envisioned as a profane activity. As we noted previously, not every act of killing is considered sacrificial in the Hebrew Bible (see above, p. 28). Even the Hebrew term *'āšām* in verse 10, which is customarily translated as "guilt offering," is in this context probably not employed as a technical term from the sacrificial cult. According to a recent exegetical consensus, it rather conveys that guilt is vicariously borne by an innocent party and thus eliminated.[178] For the story of Jesus in the Gospel according to John, this means that innocent suffering and eventually a vicarious death can be articulated in noncultic interpretive categories.

In John's passion narrative, the crucified Jesus dies on the afternoon before the Feast of Passover, that is, at the traditional time when the Passover lambs were slaughtered. This timing suggests that Jesus is a Passover lamb. Indeed, such an understanding is made explicit by Paul when he calls Christ a "Passover (lamb)" that "has been slaughtered" (1 Cor 5:7). The Revelation of John uses the reference "lamb" (Greek *arnion*) no less than twenty-nine times as a synonym for Jesus Christ. Sometimes this predication is expanded through the words "as if (it had been) slaughtered" (Rev 5:6; see also 13:8).

What then is the significance of Passover? Its earliest form in the Hebrew Bible is connected to Israel's exodus from Egypt. Here, the Passover appears as a celebration that in fact required that a lamb be slaughtered by a household community (Exod 12:6). The lamb was to be roasted over the fire and completely eaten by the community. Its blood was then applied to the lintel and the two doorposts of the houses of the Israelites (Exod 12:22). It served as a visible sign that protected Israel from the punishment that was soon to come over Egypt; because of this signal, the tenth plague was to literally "pass over" Israel. With its specific purpose, the Passover is an apotropaic ritual. It is no cultic sacrifice because, first, it is carried out at private homes, not at sanctuaries, and second, because no part of it is ever burned on an altar for God; instead, the entire lamb is consumed by humans.[179] For that reason, the Passover is never called an "offering [qorbān] for God" and is not counted among the cultic sacrifices in the priestly cult system.[180]

If Jesus, therefore, is called a "lamb" in a way that evokes the apotropaic tradition of the Passover, then the modus operandi of the blood application rite is not consecration or expiation. Jesus was *not* crucified on the Day of Atonement. The blood of the Passover animal does represent life, but in this case the life force has the power of shielding the human community from danger and death. Such an interpretation suits the visions of the Revelation of John, which feature dramatic cosmic battles between the forces of good and evil. In such a scenario, the blood of Christ, the Passover lamb, wards off evil and protects his followers.[181]

So far, several ancient Israelite and Judean traditions have been referenced to elucidate the origins of lamb predications. However, lambs were also used in the sacrificial cult. It is, nevertheless, peculiar that lambs were not typically offered as sin offerings (for which he-goats and sheep were characteristic; see Lev 4:23; Num 28:15, 22, 30) or as guilt offerings (for which rams were customary; see Lev 5:15-16; 6:6 [MT, LXX 5:25]). A lamb would, instead, have been readily correlated with the so-called regular burnt offering (Exod 29:38; Num 28:3). Such an association needs to be verified through the occurrence of specific cultic terminology. Indeed, Jesus is predicated in this fashion when the costliness of salvation is said to have been made possible "through the precious blood of Christ, a lamb [Greek *amnos*] without blemish or defect" (1 Pet 1:19). This motif alludes to the monetary value of sacrificial animals (see above, p. 70).

In short: The predication of Jesus as "lamb" draws on various backgrounds and has, therefore, different meanings. It may, first, describe Jesus as obedient, innocent, and weak, suggesting that he can, due to these qualities, "take away sin." Such concepts are attested in the *Rule of the Community* (1QS 8:8-10) and in the Song of the Suffering Servant (Isaiah 52:13—53:12). Other lamb motifs draw upon the apotropaic ritual of the ancient Israelite and Judean Passover tradition. Representing the force of life, the blood of Jesus, the Passover lamb, has the power of protecting a community from danger and death. Among the various lamb predications, ultimately only one passage (1 Pet 1:19) evokes the sacrificial cult. It alludes to the monetary value of sacrificial animals in order to illustrate the costliness of salvation through Jesus.

Summary: Sacrificial Metaphors Applied to Jesus

In this section, we have seen that New Testament sacrificial metaphors occur in paraenetic and christological contexts. When used with reference to Jesus Christ, some of these metaphors point to his entire life and mission, which are depicted as acceptable to God. Other terms focus on his death, which made his blood available; the latter communicates his life, which has the power of eliminating sin and consecrating humans. The phrase the "blood of Jesus," therefore, does not evince vicarious dying. Both images, however, manifest the incarnational basis of salvation.

In my interpretation of this rich spectrum of sacrificial metaphors and concepts, I suggested that each contributes a specific facet to the good news of Jesus Christ. We thus recognize the imaginative resourcefulness of early Christianity that found indeed multifaceted ways of proclaiming the gospel. I hope I have shown that it is important to familiarize ourselves with ancient Israelite/Judean traditions and practices in order to more fully appreciate the contents of these terms and motifs.

Admittedly, some of these motifs might be unfamiliar for Christians of postmodern Western culture. For example, how do we respond to the idea that the original notion of sacrifice featured in the Bible is different and has more positive connotations? Or how do we respond to the proposal that Jesus initially instituted the eucharistic cup as a consecration rite according to traditional cultic patterns? While we might consider this strange, we need to acknowledge that the classification of sin as a form of defilement remains a fixture in Western culture. This is evident when, in common parlance, expressions like "dirty thoughts" are used for improper ideas. We are probably not that far removed from the terminological and cultural conventions of ancient Judaism a few millennia ago.

Other Christological Metaphors and Concepts in the New Testament

In this section, I will discuss New Testament metaphors, concepts, and phrases that interpret or capture the salvific significance of Jesus. They are, however, not derived from sacrificial rituals; therefore, they are not cultic. They rather reference secular motifs that were prominent in the environment of early Christianity. The task of interpreting them requires that the postmodern reader reconnects these metaphors and concepts to the sociocultural matrix of the ancient Greco-Roman world. Back then, the usage of such secular images assured that the message of salvation through Jesus Christ was accessible to culturally and ethnically diverse audiences of the first century C.E.

The attentive reader might ask why a book on sacrifice and the sacrifice of Jesus discusses secular images at all. Did not the previous paragraphs cover most relevant areas of the sacrificial cult? The answer to this question lies in the ambivalent character of the term *sacrifice* in modern-day parlance. Today, this term is chiefly employed as a metaphor that has only little in common with its original usage in religious rituals.[182] It has become secularized. Specifically, this metaphorical usage of the term *sacrifice* is rather incompatible with its biblical use. It is, instead, equivalent to the modern usage of the term *atonement*, understood as a broad and abstract interpretive category for salvation through Jesus Christ.

The following paragraphs will, however, not offer any exhaustive study of secular christological metaphors and concepts due to the limited scope of this publication. It will, rather, present a rough sketch.[183]

Jesus Becomes a Curse

Temple rituals did not only comprise sacrifices. Elimination rituals such as the scapegoat (Lev 16:20-22) were also known in ancient Israel and Judah (see above, p. 90). Their equivalent in ancient Greece was the so-called *pharmakos* ritual. The apostle Paul makes reference to these archaic rituals when he writes: "Christ redeemed us from the curse of the law by becoming a curse for us" (Gal 3:13). He thus conveys the innocence of Jesus and the sinfulness of humans who cannot free themselves from their existential bondage. Salvation then occurs as existential exchange: Christ shared the human predicament, while humans participate in his holiness and glory. A similar exchange is envisioned when Paul writes: "God made him who had no sin to be sin for us, so that in him we might become the righteousness of God" (2 Cor 5:21).

For the sake of clarification, I would like to repeat that scapegoat rituals are not to be confused with cultic sacrifices; they have diametrically opposite dynamics.[184] Moreover, the animal used in elimination rituals is not killed. It is explicitly called "living" and is meant to escape. Thus Paul, when referencing the tradition of elimination rituals, does not focus on the death of Christ, but has his earthly ministry in mind.

Jesus Died for Us

However, there are soteriological images that clearly focus on the death of Jesus. For example, Paul writes that "God demonstrates his love for us; while we were still sinners Christ died for us" (Rom 5:8; see also John 11:50-52; 18:14; Rom 5:6; 1 Cor 8:11; 15:3; 1 Thess 5:10). Phrases like these are attested in the earliest soteriological confessions and hymns of Christianity that predate the New Testament writings. They are called "dying formulas" by scholars today. Such phrases are not metaphors but portray Christ's death as an "effective" death by ascribing meaning to it: They suggest that this death was not in vain, but made a crucial difference for humanity. They express more precisely that an existential exchange between Jesus and humans occurred. Their scriptural background may be the Song of the Suffering Servant (Isa 53:3) or stories of Judean martyrs (2 Macc 7:37-38).[185] They can therefore be considered to convey the vicarious surrender of life for others.

It should be pointed out that these New Testament phrases, while clearly referencing the death of Jesus, never dwell on its violent reality. Instead, they reference this death as briefly as possible. This corresponds with the observation that also the passion stories in the New Testament Gospels, while mentioning these brutal events, barely depict any graphic details. The torture of Jesus through flagellation, for instance, is mentioned in just a few words (Mark 15:15; John 19:1). While early Christians could not avoid the fact that Jesus had died a violent death, they certainly did not dwell on it. Rather, the fact that Jesus had died was considered to be important, not the least because without his actual death, his resurrection would be rendered moot.

Jesus Gives His Life for Us

One of the most popular and well-known statements of salvation is the following: "For God so loved the world that he gave his only Son, so that everyone who believes in him may not perish but may have eternal life" (John 3:16). Some people today consider it so important and central to the Christian message that they hold up signs in sports arenas that mention only the Bible reference of this passage. Statements and phrases similar to this one can be found in, for instance, Mark 10:45 and Romans 4:25.

The phrase that Jesus "gave [Greek *paradidomi*] his life for you/us" (Eph 5:2; see also Rom 8:32; Titus 2:14) expresses related ideas. Either formula is often understood as a parallel to the dying formula. But do they really always reference Christ's death? This is definitely the appropriate understanding of Romans 4:25, where both Christ's death *and* his resurrection are said to have soteriological significance.

Luke, however, writes that, after the apostles' council, some men were chosen to share the council's decisions with various Christian congregations. It is interesting that these "postmen" are introduced as having "given [Greek *paradidomi*] their lives for the name of our Lord Jesus Christ" (Acts 15:26). The instance affirms that these formulas do not refer exclusively to the death of somebody; the apostles did not select deceased people as postmen. Instead, such formulas refer in a wider sense to the perils of a special assignment and the courage of those willing to engage in it. When applied to Jesus, these formulas equally convey that he did not live the life of Riley but went on a dangerous mission. He sympathized with the poor, outcast, and marginalized of his society and publicly questioned both political standards and religious authorities of his day through acts of deliberate provocation. His goal was to bring about change for the better of humanity. This resulted in an ever-escalating conflict and, ultimately, in his execution for charges of sedition and treason.[186] Formulas that Jesus "gave his life," then, really mean that he "put his life on the line." They certainly include the extreme of death, but are not limited to it. Their contents are thus similar to those phrases regarding risking one's life for one's friends (John 15:13; see also John 10:11, 15).

The Eucharistic Image of the Body of Jesus

The Synoptic Gospels mention that, during the celebration of the Last Supper, Jesus shared bread and wine with his disciples. He took a loaf of bread and blessed it. After breaking it, he gave it to the disciples, saying: "Take; this is my body" (Mark 14:22). He then also gave them the cup with wine. While the words Jesus spoke over the latter have cultic connotations (see above, pp. 109–11), the sharing of the bread is a secular motif. In general, bread is both a basic (Matt 6:11) and omnipresent staple in ancient cultural and biblical contexts. Its metaphorical meaning conveys its fundamental role for human existence. Jesus therefore called himself the "bread of life" (John 6:35), and bread was also at the center of the feeding miracles (Mark 6:30-44; 8:1-9; John 6:1-15). Thus, bread represents, on the one hand, core scenes of the ministry of Jesus for those in need. Jesus had launched a reform movement that promoted the ideal of an inclusive society across traditional boundaries. This ideal was particularly communicated during meals (Mark 2:13-17). On the other hand, bread was explicitly identified with Jesus. When the disciples ate the bread that Jesus gave them, they understood it as a representation of him that referred to his entire ministry on behalf of others. When eating it, the disciples understood that they, too, were sustained through his ministry. At the same time, the fact that the bread was broken conveyed, once more, the impending death of Jesus.

Reconciliation

A characteristic soteriological feature of Pauline (and deutero-Pauline) writings is the concept of reconciliation. The apostle can, for example, articulate salvation as follows: "For if, while we were enemies, we were reconciled to God through the death of his Son, much more certainly, having been reconciled, we will be saved by his life" (Rom 5:10; see also 2 Cor 5:18-20; Eph 2:16; Col 1:20, 22). Paul here uses a Hellenistic concept from the secular realm of ancient diplomacy. It is usually communicated through the Greek lexeme *katallassō*.[187]

The concept of reconciliation evidently describes salvation through Christ's death. It implies that relationships between estranged parties have been restored. The one who mediates between these parties, however, risks his life. Given the importance of military endeavors in the Greco-Roman world, this soteriological motif was accessible to a diverse audience. It is not surprising that this specific terminology occurs in letters sent to urban centers in ancient Italy, Greece, and Asia Minor.

Redemption

Finally, secular interpretive categories are chosen when Jesus is reported to have said: "For the Son of Man came not to be served but to serve, and to give his life a ransom for many" (Mark 10:45; see also Matt 20:28). The Greek term for "ransom" is *lytron*; it refers to deliverance from the existential bondage under debt, while the ransom price is Christ's life or blood. It is assumed that the human debt cannot simply be canceled but must be fully paid. If necessary, somebody else has to make the payment. Therefore, this interpretive category conveys the vicarious surrender of life for others.

Further Greek terms belonging to this concept are *apolytrōsis*, "redemption"; *lytroōmai*, "to redeem" (Rom 3:24; Eph 1:7; 1 Pet 1:18); and *(ex) agorazō*, "to redeem/purchase" (1 Cor 6:20; Gal 3:13; 4:5; 2 Pet 2:1; Rev 5:9). Ransom and redemption are mercantile terms. They typically refer to money paid for the release of slaves or captives. Considering that a large percentage of the population in the ancient Greco-Roman world was slaves, this soteriological concept was intelligible to many. Its imagery must have strongly resonated with those at the bottom of society. In terms of outcome, it conveys liberation and a critical upgrade of one's status within the social hierarchy.

Summary

In short, the previous paragraphs show that early Christianity articulated the salvific significance of Jesus not only through metaphors, concepts, and phrases derived from the temple cult but also through those pointing to different secular backgrounds such as economics or diplomacy. All of them agree that Jesus or God is in charge of salvation and that it is effective. All of them should, nevertheless, be assessed individually in order to grasp their diverse contents and what exactly they convey: Some of these metaphors and phrases refer to the life of Jesus (curse), others refer to his death (dying formulas, reconciliation, redemption), others can refer to both ("Jesus gives his live for us"). Some of these secular motifs do assume a vicarious death for humans (dying formulas, redemption).

3

Conclusions

Rethinking the "Sacrifice of Jesus"

In this study on the sacrifice of Jesus, I have investigated core symbols of Christianity. Salvation through Jesus Christ is often articulated through the concept of sacrifice. Yet many today have trouble accepting this concept, as it seems to convey death, violence, and the image of a vengeful and implacable God. These caveats pertain not only to the cognitive perception of biblical texts or church doctrine but also to how Christians understand the liturgical celebration of the Eucharist, or Last Supper, the climactic element of Christian worship, which makes salvation accessible in an emotive fashion.

In response to what might be labeled a Christian identity crisis, I have first investigated the sacrificial cult within its context as it emerges from the texts of the Hebrew Bible. I have, second, studied the New Testament concept of the sacrifice of Jesus in its light. In the course of this investigation, I have argued the following:

1. There has been a tendency to portray all central rituals of the ancient Israelite/Judean cult as functioning through death or killing. This has led some to assume that the very center of Israelite/Judean worship was occupied by an institution bent on the annihilation of life, and that Levitical priests were first of all "butchers." Religion and even sacredness were, therefore, easily coupled with violence. Against such interpretations, I have argued that the importance of killing is strongly overrated in modern theories of sacrifice. On the one hand, *animal slaughter* had *no special* and certainly *no constitutive significance* for sacrificial rituals of the ancient Israelite/Judean cult. This is exemplified through the observation that the cereal offering is a cultic sacrifice that "functions" without a victim. On the other hand, cultic *blood application rituals* do not enact vicarious death but *consecrate through the animal's life*, which is in its blood.

2. A more appropriate view is achieved when one considers the complex nature of sacrificial rituals (polythetic approach) and takes into account the interpretive comments featured in priestly regulations. Such an approach reveals apportionment as central to sacrifice and the burning rite on the altar of burnt offering as its constitutive component. Sacrificial rituals of ancient Israel and Judah then emerge as ways of *approaching the sanctuary* with the goal of *encountering* and *communicating with God*. In addition, sacrifices are means of *cultic purification and consecration* (expiation).

3. Common Christian views of the sacrificial cult as it is depicted in the Hebrew Bible demand rehabilitation. This important task has *significant ramifications* for how Christians understand the metaphors derived from this cult: many christological and soteriological concepts and images appear in a different light and have more positive implications. Most important is the discovery that, according to the New Testament, Christ's entire mission and life have salvific value. *New Testament soteriology* does not focus exclusively on the death of Jesus but *includes his life and mission.* It corresponds to the message of the early secret symbol of Christianity, the fish (Greek *ichthys*): As an acrostic, it expresses that Jesus, who is the Christ and the Son of God, is the savior—not only that his death effects salvation. Modern views of atonement should be *broadened* to reflect these aspects of early Christian soteriology.

4. The early Christian church understood *Christ's death on the cross as salvific.* The exclusive soteriological value of this event is, however, primarily *expressed* through metaphors and phrases *derived from secular contexts* such as economics or diplomacy. Today such metaphors and phrases are frequently subsumed under broader notions of sacrifice and atonement. Originally, however, these secular interpretive categories did not belong to the sacrificial cult.

5. In many perceptions of the sacrifice of Jesus and atonement, God often appears as a cruel and wrathful divine father who must be appeased through the death of an innocent

person. According to early Christian theology, however, *God* took the *initiative of putting forth Jesus as the "place of atonement"* that is accessible for all humans, and *God* was the one who *reconciled the world* by providing humans with an effective means of forgiveness. In Jesus, the triune God chose to encounter humanity so that the *divine love* could be recognized and shared with the world.

The concept of the sacrifice of Jesus, then, invites people to accept the salvation that God has prepared for humanity. This salvation is experienced in the celebration with bread and wine. It allows Christians to become agents of love and peace by being reconciled first to God and then to one another.

Glossary of Cultic Terminology in the Hebrew Bible and the New Testament

1. אֹהֶל מוֹעֵד (*'ohel mô'ēd*)—tent of meeting (tabernacle)
2. אָשָׁם (*'āšām*)—A. guilt; B. guilt offering
3. אִשֶּׁה (*'iššeh*)—offering by fire
4. דָּם (*dām*)—blood
5. זבח (*zabaḥ*)—to slaughter; to sacrifice (with reference to the entire ritual)
6. זֶבַח (*zebaḥ*)—sacrifice
7. זֶבַח שְׁלָמִים (*zebaḥ šĕlāmîm*)—sacrifice of well-being
8. זרק (*zaraq*)—to dash (toss)
9. חַטָּאת (*ḥaṭṭa't*)—A. sin; B. sin offering
10. יוֹם הַכִּפֻּרִים (*yôm hakkippurîm*)—Day of Atonement
11. כַּפֹּרֶת (*kappōret*)—Mercy Seat (cover of the Ark of the Covenant)
12. כִּפֶּר (*kipper*)—to atone
13. מִזְבֵּחַ (*mizbeaḥ*)—altar
14. מִזְבֵּחַ הָעֹלָה (*mizbâḥ ha'ōlâ*)—altar of burnt offering
15. מִנְחָה (*minḥâ*)—A. *general*: tribute; B. *cultic*: sacrifice; cereal offering
16. סמך (*sāmak*)—to lean (one's hand)
17. עֹלָה (*'ōlâ*)—burnt offering (literally: rising up)
18. עֹלַת תָּמִיד (*'ōlat tāmîd*)—continuous sacrifice
19. קטר (*qaṭar*); *hiph'il* stem: הִקְטִיר—to burn (on the altar); also: to turn into smoke

20. קָרַב (*qarab*); *hiph'il* stem: הִקְרִיב–to offer, to bring near

21. קָרְבָּן (*qorbān*)–offering (literally: what is brought near)

22. קָרְבָּן לַיהוָה (*qorbān l'Adonai*)–offering for Y<small>HWH</small>

23. רֵיחַ־נִיחוֹחַ (*rêaḥ-nîḥôaḥ*)–pleasing odor

24. שָׂרַף (*śarap*)–to burn (no cultic relevance; for purpose of destruction)

25. שָׁחַט (*šaḥaṭ*)–to slaughter (by cutting the throat of an animal)

Greek Terms

1. αἷμα (*haima*)–blood

2. δῶρον (*dōron*)–gift

3. εἰς ὀσμὴν εὐωδίας (*eis osmēn euōdias*)–for a pleasing odor

4. θυμιατήριον (*thymiatērion*)–censer

5. θυσία (*thysia*)–sacrifice

6. θυσιαστήριον (*thysiastērion*)–altar

7. θύω (*thyō*)–to offer, to sacrifice (originally: to burn); to slaughter, to slay

8. ἱλασμός (*hilasmos*)–atonement

9. ἱλαστήριον (*hilastērion*)–place of (means of) atonement

10. ὁλοκαύτωμα (*holokautōma*)–whole burnt offering

11. προσφέρω (*prospherō*)–to offer, to sacrifice (literally: to bring near)

12. προσφορά (*prosphora*)–offering

Abbreviations

ABD	*Anchor Bible Dictionary.* Edited by D. N. Freedman. 6 vols. New York: Doubleday, 1992.
AncB	*Anchor Bible*
ANRW	*Aufstieg und Niedergang der römischen Welt: Geschichte und Kultur Roms im Spiegel der neueren Forschung.* Edited by H. Temporini and W. Haase. Berlin, 1972–
ASoc	*l'Année sociologique*
BEHE.R	Bibliothèque de l'École des Hautes Études, Sciences Religieuses
BWA(N)T	Beiträge zur Wissenschaft vom Alten (und Neuen) Testament
BibInt	*Biblical Interpretation*
BibInt.S	Biblical Interpretation Series
BK.AT	Biblischer Kommentar, Altes Testament. Edited by M. Noth and H. W. Wolff
CBOTS	*Coniectanea biblica: Old Testament series*
CC	Continental Commentaries
DSD	*Dead Sea Discoveries*
EnAC	Entretiens sur l'antiquité classique
EvTh	*Evangelische Theologie*
FRLANT	Forschungen zur Religion und Literatur des Alten und Neuen Testaments
FS	Festschrift
HSM	Harvard Semitic Monographs

IEJ	*Israel Exploration Journal*
HTR	*Harvard Theological Review*
JAOS	*Journal of the American Oriental Society*
JBL	*Journal of Biblical Literature*
JSNT	*Journal for the Study of the New Testament*
JSNT.S	Journal for the Study of the New Testament: Supplement Series
JSOT	*Journal for the Study of the Old Testament*
KuD	Kerygma und Dogma
LHBOTS	Library of Hebrew Bible/Old Testament Studies
NovT	*Novum Testamentum*
NTS	*New Testament Studies*
Numen	*Numen: International Review for the History of Religions*
OBO	Orbis biblicus et orientalis
ÖTBK	Ökumenischer Taschenbuchkommentar
OTL	Old Testament Library
PEQ	*Palestine Exploration Quarterly*
RelSRev	*Religious Studies Review*
RGG	*Religion in Geschichte und Gegenwart.* Edited by K. Galling. 7 vols. 3rd ed. Tübingen, 1957–65
SBL.SP	*Society of Biblical Literature Seminar Papers*
SBS	Stuttgarter Bibelstudien
SOTSMS	Society for Old Testament Studies Monograph Series
TANZ	Texte und Arbeiten zum neutestamentlichen Zeitalter
ThZ	*Theologische Zeitschrift*

TRE	*Theologische Realenzyklopädie.* Edited by G. Krause and G. Müller. Berlin, 1977–2004
TynB	*Tyndale Bulletin*
VT.S	Supplements to Vetus Testamentum
WMANT	Wissenschaftliche Monographien zum Alten und Neuen Testament
WUNT	Wissenschaftliche Untersuchungen zum Neuen Testament
ZAW	*Zeitschrift für die alttestamentliche Wissenschaft*
ZDPV	*Zeitschrift des deutschen Palästina-Vereins*

Bibliography

T. D. Alexander, 1995, "The Passover Sacrifice," in: R. T. Beckwith/M. J. Selman (eds.), *Sacrifice in the Bible*, Carlisle/Grand Rapids: Paternoster/Baker, pp. 1–24.

G. A. Anderson, 1987, *Sacrifices and Offerings in Ancient Israel: Studies in their Social and Political Importance* (HSM 41), Atlanta: Scholars.

———, 1992, "Sacrifice and Sacrificial Offerings, Old Testament," *ABD* 5, pp. 870–86.

———, 1995, "Intentional and Unintentional Sin in the Dead Sea Scrolls," in: D. N. Freedman/D. P. Wright/A. Hurvitz (eds.), *Pomegranates and Golden Bells: Studies in Biblical, Jewish, and Near Eastern Ritual, Law, and Literature in Honor of Jacob Milgrom*, Winona Lake, Ind.: Eisenbrauns, pp. 49–64.

E. Assis, 2007, "To Build or Not to Build: A Dispute between Haggai and His People (Hag 1)," in: *ZAW* 119, pp. 514–27.

———, 2008, "A Disputed Temple (Haggai 2,1–9)," in: *ZAW* 120, pp. 582–96.

———, 2009, "Psalm 127 and the Polemic of the Rebuilding of the Temple in the Post Exilic Period," in: *ZAW* 121, pp. 256–72.

G. Aulén, 1953, *Christus Victor: An Historical Study of the Three Main Types of the Idea of the Atonement* (translated by A. G. Hebert), London: S.P.C.K.

J. van Baal, 1976, "Offering, Sacrifice and Gift," in: *Numen* 23, pp. 161–78.

K. C. W. F. Bähr, 1837, 1839, *Symbolik des Mosaischen Cultus*, Vol. 1, 2: Heidelberg: Mohr.

W. B. Barrick, 1992, "High Place," *ABD* 3, pp. 196–200.

J. M. Baumgarten, 1953, "Sacrifice and Worship among the Jewish Sectarians of the Dead Sea (Qumran) Scrolls," in: *HTR* 46, pp. 141–59.

———, 1999, "Yom Kippur in the Qumran Scrolls and Second Temple Sources," in: *DSD* 6, pp. 185–91.

R. T. Beckwith, 1995a, "Sacrifice in the World of the New Testament," in: idem/M. J. Selman (eds.), *Sacrifice in the Bible*, Carlisle/Grand Rapids: Paternoster/Baker, pp. 105–10.

———, 1995b, "The Death of Christ as a Sacrifice in the Teaching of Paul and Hebrews," in: idem/M. J. Selman (eds.), *Sacrifice in the Bible*, Carlisle/Grand Rapids: Paternoster/Baker, pp. 130–35.

L. A. Berman, 1997, *The Akedah: The Binding of Isaac*, Northvale/Jerusalem: Jason Aronson.

J. Blenkinsopp, 2000, *Isaiah 1–39: A New Translation with Introduction and Commentary* (AncB 19), New Haven/London: Yale University Press.

———, 2002, *Isaiah 40–55: A New Translation with Introduction and Commentary* (AncB 19A), New Haven/London: Yale University Press.

K. Bodner, 2008, *1 Samuel: A Narrative Commentary* (Hebrew Bible Monographs 19), Sheffield: Sheffield Phoenix.

C. Breytenbach, 1989, *Versöhnung: Eine Studie zur paulinischen Soteriologie* (WMANT 60), Neukirchen-Vluyn: Neukirchener.

G. J. Brooke, 2005, "The Ten Temples in the Dead Sea Scrolls," in: J. Day (ed.), *Temple and Worship in Biblical Israel* (LHBOTS 422), London/New York: T&T Clark, pp. 416–34.

R. E. Brown, 1982, *The Epistles of John: Translated, with Introduction, Notes, and Commentary* (AncB 30), New Haven/London: Yale University Press.

W. Brueggemann, 1997, *Theology of the Old Testament: Testimony, Dispute, Advocacy*, Minneapolis: Fortress Press.

D. Büchner, 2010, "Ἐξιλάσασθαι: Appeasing God in the Septuagint Pentateuch," in: *JBL* 129, pp. 237-60.

W. Burkert, 1981, "Glaube und Verhalten: Zeichengehalt und Wirkungsmacht von Opferritualen," in: J. Rudhardt/O. Reverdin (eds.), *Le sacrifice dans l'Antiquité* (EnAC 27), Vandœuvres-Genève: Fondation Hardt, pp. 91–125.

———, 1983, *Homo Necans: The Anthropology of Ancient Greek Sacrificial Ritual and Myth* (translated by P. Bing), Berkeley: University of California Press.

———, 1985, *Greek Religion* (translated by J. Raff), Cambridge: Harvard University Press.

———, 2009, *Kulte des Altertums: Biologische Grundlagen der Religion*, München: Beck (2nd edition).

B. S. Childs, 2002, *Biblical Theology: A Proposal* (Facets), Minneapolis: Fortress Press.

K. W. Clark, 1959/60, Worship in the Jerusalem Temple after AD 70, in: *NTS* 6, pp. 269–80.

M. Cogan, 2001, *I Kings: A New Translation with Introduction and Commentary* (AncB 10), New York/London: Doubleday.

M. Cogan/H. Tadmor, 1988, *II Kings: A New Translation with Introduction and Commentary* (AncB 11), New York/London: Doubleday.

F. H. Cortez, 2006, "From the Holy to the Most Holy Place: The Period of Hebrews 9:6-10 and the Day of Atonement as a Metaphor of Transition," in: *JBL* 125, pp. 527–47

R. J. Daly, 1978, *Christian Sacrifice* (Studies in Christian Antiquity 18), Washington, D.C.: Catholic University of America Press.

J. Day, 2005, "Whatever Happened to the Ark of the Covenant?" in: idem (ed.), *Temple and Worship in Biblical Israel* (LHBOTS 422), London/New York: T&T Clark, pp. 250–70.

M. Detienne, 1977, *Dionysos mis à mort*, Paris: Gallimard.

———, 1979, "Pratiques culinaires et esprit de sacrifice," in: idem/J.-P. Vernant (eds.), *La cuisine du sacrifice en pays grec*, Paris: Gallimard, pp. 7–35.

R. de Vaux, 1991, *Les Institutions de l'Ancien Testament 2: Institutions Militaires, Institutions Religieuses*, Paris: Cerf (5th edition).

B. W. V. Dombrowski, 1976, "Killing in Sacrifice: The Most Profound Experience of God?" in: *Numen* 23, pp. 136–44.

H.-M. Döpp, 1998, *Die Deutung der Zerstörung Jerusalems und des Zweiten Tempels im Jahre*

70 in den ersten drei Jahrhunderten n. Chr.
(TANZ 24), Tübingen/Basel: Francke.

M. Douglas, 2003, "The Go-Away Goat," in: R. A.
Kugler/R. Rendtorff (eds.), *The Book of Leviti-
cus: Composition and Reception* (VT.S 93),
Leiden/Boston: Brill, pp. 121–41.

D. J. Downs, 2006, "'The Offering of the Gentiles'
in Romans 15.16," in: *JSNT* 29, pp. 173–86.

B. Dücker, 2007, *Rituale: Formen–Funktionen–
Geschichte: Eine Einführung in die Ritualwis-
senschaft*, Stuttgart/Weimar: Metzler.

C. Eberhart, 2002a, *Studien zur Bedeutung der
Opfer im Alten Testament: Die Signifikanz von
Blut- und Verbrennungsriten im kultischen
Rahmen* (WMANT 94), Neukirchen-Vluyn:
Neukirchener Verlag.

———, 2002b, "Beobachtungen zum Verbren-
nungsritus bei Schlachtopfer und Gemein-
schafts-Schlachtopfer," in: *Biblica* 83, pp.
88–96.

———, 2004, "A Neglected Feature of Sacrifice in
the Hebrew Bible: Remarks on the Burning Rite
on the Altar," in: *HTR* 97, pp. 485–93.

———, 2005a, "Characteristics of Sacrificial
Metaphors in Hebrews," in: G. Gelardini (ed.),
Hebrews: Contemporary Methods, New Insights
(BibInt.S 75), Leiden/Boston: Brill, pp. 37–64.

———, 2005b, "The 'Passion' of Gibson: Evaluat-
ing a Recent Interpretation of Christ's Suffering
and Death in Light of the New Testament," in:
Consensus 30/1 (2005), pp. 37–74.

———, 2006a, "The Term 'Sacrifice' and the Problem of Theological Abstraction: A Study of the

Reception History of Genesis 22:1-19," in: C. Helmer (ed.), *The Multivalence of Biblical Texts and Theological Meanings* (Symposium Series 37), Atlanta: Society of Biblical Literature, pp. 47–66.

———, 2006b, "Schlachtung/Schächtung," *Wissenschaftliches Bibellexikon im Internet*, Stuttgart: Deutsche Bibelgesellschaft (http://www.wibilex.de; accessed: 06.05.2010).

———, 2010, "Qorban," *Wissenschaftliches Bibellexikon im Internet*, Stuttgart: Deutsche Bibelgesellschaft (http://www.wibilex.de; accessed: 25.06.2010).

———, 2011a, "Atonement. I. Old Testament/ Hebrew Bible," *Encyclopedia of the Bible and its Reception* 3, Berlin/New York: Walter De Gruyter (in print).

———, 2011b, "Atonement. III. New Testament," *Encyclopedia of the Bible and its Reception* 3, Berlin/New York: Walter De Gruyter (in print).

———, 2011c, "Blood. I. Ancient Near East and Hebrew Bible/Old Testament," *Encyclopedia of the Bible and its Reception* 4, Berlin/New York: Walter De Gruyter (in print).

———, 2011d, "Expiation," *Encyclopedia of the Bible and Its Reception*, Berlin/New York: Walter De Gruyter (forthcoming).

B. D. Ehrman, 2004, *The New Testament: A Historical Introduction to the Early Christian Writings*, New York/Oxford: Oxford University Press (3rd edition).

J. D. K. Ekem, 2007, "A Dialogical Exegesis of Romans 3.25a," in: *JSNT* 30, pp. 75–93.

E. Ferguson, 1980, "Spiritual Sacrifice in Early Christianity and its Environment," in: *ANRW* 2/23/2, pp. 1151–89.

S. Finlan, 2004, *Background and Contents of Paul's Cultic Atonement Metaphors* (Academia Biblica 19), Atlanta: Society of Biblical Literature.

———, 2005, *Problems with Atonement: The Origins of, and Controversy about, the Atonement Doctrine*, Collegeville, Minn.: Liturgical.

J. R. Frazer, 1994, *The Golden Bough: A Study in Magic and Religion*, Oxford: Oxford University Press.

J. Frey, 2005, "Probleme der Deutung des Todes Jesu in der neutestamentlichen Wissenschaft: Streiflichter zur exegetischen Diskussion," in: idem/J. Schröter (eds.), 2005, *Deutungen des Todes Jesu im Neuen Testament* (WUNT 181), Tübingen: Mohr Siebeck, pp. 3–50.

N. H. Gadegaard, 1978, "On the So-called Burnt Offering Altar in the Old Testament," in: *PEQ* 110, pp. 35–45.

O. Genest, 1988, "L'interprétation de la mort de Jésus en situation discursive," *NTS* 34, pp. 516–35.

M. K. George, 2009, *Israel's Tabernacle as Social Space* (Ancient Israel and Its Literature 2), Atlanta: Society of Biblical Literature.

H. Gese, 1981, "The Atonement," in: idem, *Essays on Biblical Theology* (translated by K. Crim), Minneapolis: Augsburg Publishing House, pp. 93–116.

J. B. Gibson, 2004, "Paul's 'Dying Formula,'" in S. E. McGinn (ed.), *Celebrating Romans*, FS R. Jewett, Grand Rapids: Eerdmans, pp. 20–41.

W. K. Gilders, 2004, *Blood Ritual in the Hebrew Bible: Meaning and Power*, Baltimore: Johns Hopkins University Press.

R. Girard, 1977, *Violence and the Sacred* (translated by Patrick Gregory), Baltimore: Johns Hopkins University Press.

———, 1979, *Des choses cachées depuis la fondation du monde*, Paris: Grasset.

———, 1987, "Generative Scapegoating," in: R. G. Hamerton-Kelly (ed.), *Violent Origins: Walter Burkert, René Girard, and Jonathan Z. Smith on Ritual Killing and Cultural Formation*, Palo Alto: Stanford University Press, pp. 73–105.

———, 1994, *Quand ces choses commenceront . . . Entretiens avec Michel Treguer,* Paris: Arléa.

M. Godelier, 1996, *L'énigme du Don*, Paris: Fayard.

M. Goodman, 2005, "The Temple in First Century CE Judaism," in: J. Day (ed.), *Temple and Worship in Biblical Israel* (LHBOTS 422), London/New York: T&T Clark, pp. 459–68.

J. A. Groves, 2004, "Atonement in Isaiah 53: 'For He Bore the Sins of Many,'" in: C. E. Hill/F. A. James III (eds.), *The Glory of the Atonement: Biblical, Historical and Practical Perspectives*, Downers Grove, Ill.: InterVarsity, pp. 61–89.

I. Gruenwald, 2003, *Rituals and Ritual Theory in Ancient Israel* (Brill Reference Library of Judaism 10), Atlanta: Society of Biblical Literature.

R. G. Hamerton-Kelly, 1992, *Sacred Violence: Paul's Hermeneutic of the Cross*, Minneapolis: Fortress Press.

M. Haran, 1963, "The Disappearance of the Ark," in: *IEJ* 13, pp. 46–58.

————, 1978, *Temples and Temple-Service in Ancient Israel: An Inquiry into Biblical Cult Phenomena and the Historical Setting of the Priestly School*, Winona Lake, Ind./Oxford: Eisenbrauns/Clarendon.

R. A. Harrisville, 2006, *Fracture: The Cross as Irreconcilable in the Language and Thought of the Biblical Writers*, Grand Rapids/Cambridge (U.K.): Eerdmans.

F. Hartenstein, 2005, "Zur symbolischen Bedeutung des Blutes im Alten Testament," in: J. Frey/J. Schröter (eds.), *Deutungen des Todes Jesu im Neuen Testament* (WUNT 181), Tübingen: Mohr Siebeck, pp. 119–37.

R. Hecht, 1982, "Studies on Sacrifice, 1970–1980," in: *RelSRev* 8, pp. 253–59.

S. M. Heim, 2006, *Saved from Sacrifice: A Theology of the Cross*, Grand Rapids: Eerdmans.

H. Hubert/M. Mauss, 1899, "Essai sur la nature et la fonction du sacrifice," in: *ASoc* 2, pp. 29–138.

V. A. Hurowitz, 1985, "The Priestly Account of Building the Tabernacle," in: *JAOS* 105, pp. 21–30.

————, 2005, "YHWH'S Exalted House—Aspects of the Design and Symbolism of Solomon's Temple," in: J. Day (ed.), *Temple and Worship in Biblical Israel* (Library of Hebrew Bible/Old Testament Studies 422), London/New York: T&T Clark, pp. 63–110.

B. Janowski, 1997, *Stellvertretung: Alttestamentliche Studien zu einem theologischen Grundbegriff* (SBS 165), Stuttgart: Katholisches Bibelwerk.

Th. W. Jennings Jr., 2009, *Transforming Atonement: A Political Theology of the Cross*, Minneapolis: Fortress Press.

P. P. Jenson, 1995, "The Levitical Sacrificial System," in: R. T. Beckwith/M. J. Selman (eds.), *Sacrifice in the Bible*, Carlisle/Grand Rapids: Paternoster, pp. 25–40.

R. Jewett, 2007, *Romans: A Commentary* (Hermeneia), Minneapolis: Fortress Press.

R. W. Johnson, 2001, *Going Outside the Camp: The Sociological Function of the Levitical Critique in the Epistle to the Hebrews* (JSNT.S 209), Sheffield: Sheffield Academic.

D. R. Jones, 1991, "Sacrifice and Holiness," in: S. W. Sykes (ed.), *Sacrifice and Redemption: Durham Essays in Theology*, Cambridge: Cambridge University Press, pp. 9–21.

M. Karrer, 2008, *Der Brief an die Hebräer: Kapitel 5,11–13,25* (ÖTBK 20/2), Gütersloh: Gütersloher.

H.-J. Klauck, 1992, "Sacrifice and Sacrificial Offerings, New Testament" (translated by R. H. Fuller), *ABD* 5, pp. 886–91.

J. Klawans, 2006, *Purity, Sacrifice, and the Temple: Symbolism and Supersessionism in the Study of Ancient Judaism*, Oxford/New York: Oxford University Press.

G. A. Klingbeil, 2006, "'Momentaufnahmen' of Israelite Religion: The Importance of the Communal Meal in Narrative Texts in I/II Regum and Their Ritual Dimension," in: *ZAW* 118, pp. 22–45.

K. Koch, 1966, "Sühne und Sündenvergebung um die Wende von der exilischen zur nachexilischen Zeit," in: *EvTh* 26, pp. 217–39.

W. Kraus, 2003, "Opfer II. Religionsgeschichtlich 5. Neues Testament und frühes Christentum," *RGG* 6 (4th edition), pp. 580–83.

———, 2008, "Der Erweis der Gerechtigkeit Gottes im Tode Jesu nach Röm 3,24-26," in: L. Doering/H.-G. Waubke/F. Wilk (eds.), *Judaistik und Neutestamentliche Wissenschaft: Standorte–Grenzen–Beziehungen* (FRLANT 226), Göttingen: Vandenhoeck & Ruprecht, pp. 192–216.

S. Kreuzer, 2007, "Lade JHWHs/Bundeslade," *Wissenschaftliches Bibellexikon im Internet*, Stuttgart: Deutsche Bibelgesellschaft (http://www.wibilex.de; accessed: 10.01.2010).

X. Léon-Dufour, 1982, *Le partage du pain eucharistique selon le Nouveau Testament*, Paris: Éditions du Seuil.

M. Leuchter, 2005, "The Temple Sermon and the Term מקום in the Jeremianic Corpus," in: *JSOT* 30, pp. 93–109.

D. Lioy, 2010, *Axis of Glory: A Biblical and Theological Analysis of the Temple Motif in Scripture* (Studies in Biblical Literature 138), New York: Peter Lang.

J.-C. Margueron, 1991, "L'espace sacrificiel dans le proche-orient ancien," in: R. Étienne/M.-Th. Le Dinahet (eds.), *L'espace sacrificiel dans les civilisations méditerranéennes de l'antiquité: Actes du Colloque tenu à la Maison de l'Orient, Lyon, 4–7 juin 1988* (Publications de la Bibliothèque Salomon-Reinach 5), Paris: Diffusion de Boccard, pp. 235–42.

A. Marx, 1994, *Les offrandes végétales dans l'Ancien Testament: Du tribut d'hommage au repas*

eschatologique (VT.S 57), Leiden/New York/
Köln: Brill.

———, 2005, *Les systèmes sacrificiels de l'Ancien
Testament: Formes et fonctions du culte sacrificiel à Yhwh* (VT.S 105), Leiden/Boston: Brill.

———, 2006, "Tuer, donner, manger dans le culte
sacrificiel de l'ancien Israël," in: S. Georgoudi/R.
Koch Piettre/F. Schmidt (eds.), *La cuisine et
l'autel: Les sacrifices en questions dans les
sociétés de la Méditerranée ancienne* (BEHE.R
124), Turnhout: Brepols, pp. 3–13.

A. Marx/C. Grappe, 1998, *Le sacrifice: Vocation
et subversion du sacrifice dans les deux Testa-
ments* (EssBib 29), Genève: Labor et Fides.

K. McClymond, 2008, *Beyond Sacred Violence:
A Comparative Study of Sacrifice*, Baltimore:
Johns Hopkins University Press.

S. McKnight, 2005, *Jesus and His Death: Histori-
ography, the Historical Jesus, and Atonement
Theory*, Waco: Baylor University Press.

B. H. McLean, 1991, "Christ as a Pharmakos in
Pauline Soteriology," in: *SBL.SP*, pp. 187–206.

———, 1992, "The Absence of an Atoning Sacrifice in Paul's Soteriology," in: *NTS* 38, pp.
531–53.

J. Milgrom, 1991, *Leviticus 1–16: A New Translation with Introduction and Commentary* (AncB
3A), New York/London: Doubleday.

———, 1996, "Further on the Expiatory Sacrifices," in: *JBL* 115, pp. 511–14.

———, 2000, *Leviticus 17–22: A New Translation with Introduction and Commentary* (AncB
3B), New York/London: Doubleday.

————, 2004, *Leviticus: A Book of Ritual and Ethics* (CC), Minneapolis: Fortress Press.

M. Modéus, 2005, *Sacrifice and Symbol: Biblical Š l mîm in a Ritual Perspective* (CBOTS 52), Stockholm: Almqvist & Wiksell International.

D. M. Moffitt, 2006, "Righteous Bloodshed, Matthew's Passion Narrative, and the Temple's Destruction: Lamentations as a Matthean Intertext," in: *JBL* 125, pp. 299–320.

M. Neusch, 1995, "Une conception chrétienne du sacrifice: Le modèle de Saint Augustin," in: idem (ed.), *Le sacrifice dans les religions* (Sciences théologiques et religieuses 3), Paris: Beauchesne, pp. 117–38.

J. Neusner, 1978, *A History of the Mishnaic Law of Holy Things.* Vol. 1: Zebahim, Leiden: Brill.

E. Nicole, 2004, "Atonement in the Pentateuch: 'It is the Blood That Makes Atonement for One's Life,'" in: C. E. Hill/F. A. James III (eds.), *The Glory of the Atonement: Biblical, Historical and Practical Perspectives* (FS R. Nicole), Downers Grove, Ill.: InterVarsity, pp. 35–50.

W. Palaver, 2008, *René Girards mimetische Theorie: Im Kontext kulturtheoretischer und gesellschaftspolitischer Fragen* (Beiträge zur mimetischen Theorie 6), Münster: LIT (3rd edition).

R. Rendtorff, 1967, *Studien zur Geschichte des Opfers im Alten Israel* (WMANT 24), Neukirchen-Vluyn: Neukirchener.

————, 2004, *Leviticus Vol. 1. Leviticus 1,1–10,20* (BK.AT 3), Neukirchen-Vluyn: Neukirchener.

C. Rowland, 2005, "The Temple in the New Testament," in: J. Day (ed.), *Temple and Worship in Biblical Israel* (LHBOTS 422), London/New York: T&T Clark, pp. 469–83.

C. Schlund, 2005, "Deutungen des Todes Jesu im Rahmen der Pesach-Tradition," in: J. Frey/J. Schröter (eds.), *Deutungen des Todes Jesu im Neuen Testament* (WUNT 181), Tübingen: Mohr Siebeck, pp. 397–411.

R. Schwager, 1985, "Christ's Death and the Prophetic Critique of Sacrifice," in: A. J. McKenna (ed.), *René Girard and Biblical Studies* (Semeia 33), Decatur, Ga.: Scholars, pp. 109–23.

J. Sklar, 2005, *Sin, Impurity, Sacrifice, Atonement: The Priestly Conceptions*, Sheffield: Sheffield Phoenix.

B. D. Sommer, 2001, "Conflicting Constructions of Divine Presence in the Priestly Tabernacle," in: *BibInt* 9, pp. 41–63.

H. Spieckermann, 2001, "Stellvertretung II. Altes Testament," *TRE* 32, Berlin/New York: Walter de Gruyter, pp. 135–37.

S. Stanley, 1995, "Hebrews 9:6-10: The 'Parable' of the Tabernacle," in: *NovT* 37, pp. 385–99.

———, 1994, "The Structure of Hebrews from Three Perspectives," in: *TynBul* 45, pp. 245–71.

G. Stansell, 2002, "Gifts, Tributes, and Offerings," in: W. Stegemann/B. J. Malina/G. Theissen (eds.), *The Social Setting of Jesus and the Gospels*, Minneapolis: Fortress Press, pp. 349–64.

G. Stemberger, 1995, "Opfer III. Judentum," *TRE* 25, Berlin/New York: Walter de Gruyter, pp. 267–70.

I. Strenski, 1997, "The Social and Intellectual Origins of Hubert and Mauss's Theory of Ritual Sacrifice," in: D. van der Meij (ed.), *India and*

Beyond: Aspects of Literature, Meaning, Ritual and Thought, London: Keagan Paul International, pp. 511–37.

M. A. Sweeney, 2007, *I & II Kings: A Commentary* (OTL), Louisville: Westminster John Knox.

M. Vahrenhorst, 2008, *Kultische Sprache in den Paulusbriefen* (WUNT 230), Tübingen: Mohr Siebeck.

V. Valeri, 1985, *Kingship and Sacrifice: Ritual and Society in Ancient Hawaii* (translated by Paula Wissing), Chicago: University of Chicago Press.

P. H. Vaughan, 1974, *The Meaning of "bāmâ" in the Old Testament: A Study of Etymological, Textual and Archaeological Evidence* (SOTSMS 3), Cambridge: Cambridge University Press.

J. W. Watts, 2007, *Ritual and Rhetoric in Leviticus: From Sacrifice to Scripture*, Cambridge: Cambridge University Press.

H. Weippert, 1988, *Palästina in vorhellenistischer Zeit* (Handbuch der Archäologie 2/1), München: Beck.

H. Wells, 2002, "Not Moral Heroes: The Grace of God and the Church's Public Voice," in: P. D. Airhart/M. J. Legge/Gary L. Redcliffe (eds.), *Doing Ethics in a Pluralistic World* (FS R. C. Hutchinson; Comparative Ethics Series), Waterloo, Ont.: Wilfrid Laurier University Press, pp. 77–98.

P. Welten, 1972, "Kulthöhe and Jahwetemple," in: *ZDPV* 88, pp. 19–37.

J. T. Whitney, 1979, "'Bamoth' in the Old Testament," in: *TynBul* 30, pp. 125–47.

P. Wick, 2002, *Die urchristlichen Gottesdienste: Entstehung und Entwicklung im Rahmen der frühjüdischen Tempel-, Synagogen- und Hausfrömmigkeit* (BWA[N]T 150), Stuttgart: Kohlhammer.

I. Wilson, 2005, "Merely a Container? The Ark in Deuteronomy," in: J. Day (ed.), *Temple and Worship in Biblical Israel* (LHBOTS 422), London/New York: T&T Clark, pp. 212–49.

G. R. H. Wright, 1971, "Pre-Israelite Temples in the Land of Canaan," in: *PEQ* 103, pp. 17–32.

R. K. Yerkes, 1952, *Sacrifice in Greek and Roman Religions and Early Judaism*, New York: Scribner.

R. Zimmermann, 2000, "Metapherntheorie und biblische Bildersprache: Ein methodologischer Versuch," in: *ThZ* 56, pp. 108–33.

———, 2005, "Die neutestamentliche Deutung des Todes Jesu als Opfer: Zur christologischen Koinzidenz von Opfertheologie und Opferkritik," in: *KuD* 51, pp. 72–99.

W. Zwickel, 1993, "Zur Frühgeschichte des Brandopfers in Israel," in: idem (ed.), *Biblische Welten* (FS M. Metzger; OBO 123), Freiburg (Switzerland): Universitäts-Verlag/Göttingen: Vandenhoeck & Ruprecht, pp. 231–48.

Notes

1. Tertullian, *De Corona* 3.

2. The four Gospels of Matthew, Mark, Luke, and John that have become part of the New Testament differ particularly with regard to the infancy story of Jesus (Mark and John do not feature any), various other aspects of his life story such as how many miracles Jesus performed and whether he exorcized demons (John does not recount any exorcisms), the question of how clearly Jesus claimed to be the incarnate God on earth, and the resurrection events. These differences might be due in part to the different perspectives and characteristic opinions (theologies) of the four authors (or groups of authors) who compiled and eventually wrote down their stories of Jesus at different time periods (probably between 65 and 100 c.e.) and in different locations of the ancient Mediterranean world.

3. 2006, p. 3. See also ibid., pp. 20, 23 e.a.

4. According to the article "New Survey Examines the Impact of Gibson's 'Passion' Movie," *The Barna Update*, published July 10, 2004, http://www.barna.org/barna-update/article/5-barna-update/191-new-survey-examines-the-impact-of-gibsons-qpassionq-movie, accessed January 4, 2010.

5. According to the Wikipedia article *The Passion of the Christ*, http://en.wikipedia.org/wiki/The_Passion_of_the_Christ, accessed May 20, 2010.

6. Frey, 2005, p. 8.

7. Finlan, 2005, p. 1.

8. Cf. Grappe/Marx, 1998, pp. 9–11.

9. More objections to the concepts of sacrifice and atonement can be found in, for example, Finlan, 2005, pp. 1–3; Zimmermann, 2005, pp. 73–75; Heim, 2006, pp. 21–29.

10. The person, a Lutheran Christian, was, at the time, twenty-seven years old and wanted to remain anonymous but nevertheless allowed me to use the statement. The German original of the statement is: "Die traditionelle Sühnetodlehre empfinde ich nur als abstoßend, sie ist für mich mit einem sadistischen Gottesbild verbunden. Die Sühnetodlehre hat mich lange von einem befreienden Glauben abgehalten."

11. Wells, 2002, p. 84.

12. By emphasizing that incarnation is a central and unique concept of Christianity while atonement is not, Stephen Fin-

lan opts to focus rather on *theosis*. Widely popular in Eastern Orthodox Christianity, this is the idea of deification of humanity, a process that commenced in the incarnation of Jesus Christ (Finlan, 2005, pp. 3–5, 117–24).

13. It is my experience that many Christians have a preference for the patriarchal stories in the book of Genesis and the story of Israel's exodus from Egypt, which is narrated in the first half of the book of Exodus; furthermore, the story of the Israelite kingdom in 1 Samuel–1 Kings, the prophetical books of Isaiah and Jeremiah, and finally the Psalms. Largely neglected are, among other things, the regulations governing the construction of Israel's sanctuary and the rules regarding purity and impurity and worship rituals in the second half of the book of Exodus and in Leviticus as well as Numbers. This observation is not only manifest in scholarly publications but also in popular publications. I take the liberty to mention that a children's book that I recently read to my eight-year-old son Yonas allots 215 pages to the Hebrew Bible; among these one page is dedicated to the construction of the tabernacle (plus one page of illustration), while later, six pages deal with Solomon's temple. Yet no information whatsoever is given on Israel's worship or the sacrificial rituals that were to take place at these sanctuaries. Such neglect presents a contrast to Judaism. For many centuries, the detailed regulations on cultic sacrifice in Leviticus, for example, have been the subject of learned discussion, as is manifest in the impressive number of Mishnah tracts dedicated to matters of sacrifice and temple cult (see, e.g., the tractates *Yoma; Hagigah; Zebahim; Tamid; Middot; Qinnim*).

14. Cf. Gruenwald, 2003, pp. 231, 238.

15. The trend to separate the disciplines of Hebrew Bible and New Testament continues at the academic level. Some time ago, the scholarly study of Hebrew Bible and New Testament consisted of one comprehensive discipline of biblical studies. At some point, however, the two disciplines were separated. Attempts of formulating one biblical theology were likewise abandoned; the German biblical scholar Georg Lorenz Bauer became a trailblazer when he proposed a biblical theology that was separated into an Old Testament and a New Testament component. (An easily accessible description of this development is available in Childs, 2002, pp. 4–6.) These developments have allowed scholars to pay more attention to the plethora of individual phenomena in either field of biblical studies. Yet they have not furthered the ability to recognize the continuity and connection between both areas of scholarship or between

the two parts of the biblical canon. The topic of sacrifice—and for that matter of atonement as well—requires that portions of one part of the biblical canon be seriously studied in order to be more fully understood in reference to images and concepts of the other.

16. As a disclaimer, it may be mentioned that an exhaustive treatment of the theme of atonement in the Bible is not possible due to the limited scope of this publication. For a comprehensive overview of this topic, see Finlan, 2004; idem, 2005; Eberhart, 2011a; idem, 2011b.

17. Cf. Eberhart, 2006a, p. 49.

18. This survey of scholarship is partially based on Eberhart, 2002a, pp. 187–221. For further surveys, see, e.g., Hecht, 1982, pp. 253–59; Watts, 2007, pp. 176–80.

19. German title: *Symbolik des Mosaischen Cultus.*

20. Bähr, 1839, pp. 199, 215–17.

21. Bähr, 1839, pp. 201–2.

22. *Lectures on the Religion of the Semites: The Fundamental Institutions. First Series*, London: Adam & Charles Black 1889; second edition by J. S. Black (1894).

23. Smith, 1969, p. 345.

24. Frazer, *The Golden Bough: A Study in Magic and Religion.*

25. French title: *Essai sur la nature et la fonction du sacrifice.* Ivan Strenski considered this essay to be "the most frequently cited theoretical work on sacrifice ever written" (1997, p. 511; see also Hecht, 1982, p. 256). It may be noted that the publication date of the French version of this essay is sometimes noted as 1898, sometimes as 1899. This bibliographical problem seems to be due to the circumstance that the second issue of the journal *L'Année Sociologique* in which this essay appeared was projected for 1897–98, but was in fact published in 1899.

26. Hubert/Mauss, 1899, e.g., pp. 47, 73.

27. Hubert/Mauss, 1899, pp. 36–37: "Il est bien certain, en effet, que le sacrifice implique toujours une consécration; dans tout sacrifice, un objet passe du domaine commun dans le domaine religieux; il est consacré. . . . Le fidèle qui a fourni la victime, objet de la consécration, n'est pas, à la fin de l'opération, ce qu'il était au commencement. Il a acquis un caractère religieux qu'il n'avait pas, . . . il est religieusement transformé."

28. Hubert/Mauss, 1899, pp. 67, 71–75.

29. Hubert/Mauss, 1899, pp. 66–67.

30. Hubert/Mauss, 1899, pp. 83, 133.

31. Hubert/Mauss, 1899, p. 127: "Dans tout sacrifice, la victime a quelque chose du dieu. Mais ici elle est le dieu lui-même et c'est cette identification qui caractérise le sacrifice du dieu."

32. Koch, 1966, pp. 230–31.

33. Rendtorff, 1967.

34. The English version was published in 1983 as *Homo Necans: The Anthropology of Ancient Greek Sacrificial Ritual and Myth*. The title of the 1972 German original is "Homo Necans: Interpretationen altgriechischer Opferriten und Mythen." Burkert likewise presents his theory of sacrifice in a number of subsequent publications (see the following references).

35. The English version appeared in 1977. The French original was published as *La violence et le sacré*.

36. Burkert, 1983, pp. 12–48. Burkert mentions that the moment of slaughter is emphasized through respective emotional expressions of participants in the sacrificial ritual: "As the fatal blow falls, the women must cry out in high, shrill tones: the Greek custom of the sacrificial cry marks the emotional climax. Life screams over death" (1985, p. 56; see also idem, 1983, p. 5).

37. This is already manifest in Burkert's programmatic statements in the first chapter of *Homo Necans*, titled "Sacrifice as an Act of Killing" (Burkert, 1983, pp. 1–12): "Thus, blood and violence lurk fascinatingly at the very heart of religion" (ibid., p. 2); "*Homo religiosus* acts and attains self-awareness as *homo necans*" (ibid., p. 3; see also idem, 1981, p. 109).

38. To substantiate this claim, Burkert references, on the one hand, the Lord's Supper as the "death of God's son (as) the one-time and perfect sacrifice" (Burkert, 1983, p. 8). On the other hand, he describes traditional customs of animal slaughter that survived within Christianity (ibid., pp. 8–9). Burkert concludes: "Christianity is here no more than a transparent cover for the ancient form that underlies it: that is to say, for the sacred act of blood sacrifice" (ibid., p. 9).

39. Girard, 1977, p. 55.

40. Girard, 1994, p. 29: "S'il y a un ordre normal dans les sociétés, il doit être le fruit d'une crise antérieure, il doit être la résolution de cette crise."

41. Girard, 1977, pp. 19, 93.

42. This is the title of one of Girard's books, based on Matthew 13:35; in French: *Des choses cachées depuis la fondation du monde* (1979).

43. Cf. Schwager, 1985; Hamerton-Kelly, 1992, pp. 77–81.

On Girard's interpretation of sacrifice and sacred violence, see also Gruenwald, 2003, pp. 259–62; Palaver, 2008.

44. The German original was published under the title *Die Sühne* (reprinted in H. Gese, *Zur biblischen Theologie: Alttestamentliche Vorträge*, 2nd ed.; Tübingen: Mohr Siebeck, 1983, pp. 85–106). The English translation was published in 1981.

45. Gese, 1981, p. 95.

46. Gese, 1981, p. 101.

47. Gese, 1981, p. 104. A brief note regarding the English translation of Gese's essay is in order here. The German original mentions "die Handauflegung" (e.g., p. 95), which is translated as "the laying on of hands" (Gese, 1981, e.g., p. 104). In the context of discussing this rite, Gese references Lev 1:4 (ibid., p. 103), according to which the offerer places or leans *one hand* on the head of the sacrificial animal. Gese then distinguishes this rite from that in the context of the scapegoat ritual, which is carried out with *two hands* (Lev 16:21). Since Gese assigns *different meanings* to these rites, it seems important to maintain that distinction by rendering the German term "die Handauflegung" as "the hand-leaning rite," which avoids the plural "hands."

48. Gese, 1981, pp. 114–15.

49. Gese, 1981, pp. 115–16.

50. Milgrom, 2004, p. 30: "The violation of a prohibitive commandment pollutes the sanctuary, and unless the sanctuary is purged by a purification offering the community is in danger that their God will be forced to abandon the sanctuary." Milgrom outlines his concept of graded impurity as it is manifest in Leviticus in ibid., p. 31: "If an individual has accidentally violated a prohibition, the priest purges the outer (sacrificial) altar with the blood of the offerer's purification offering ([Lev] 4:27-35). If the entire community has accidentally violated a prohibition, the priest purges the inner (incense) altar and the shrine, the outer room of the tent, with the blood of the purification offering brought by the community's representative (4:13-21). If, however, individuals have brazenly violated prohibitions, then, once a year, on Yom Kippur, the high priest purges the entire sanctuary, beginning with the inner and holiest area, containing the Ark. In this case, the purification offering is not brought by the culprits—deliberate sinners are barred from the sanctuary—but by the high priest himself."

51. Milgrom, 1991, pp. 226–318, specifically pp. 232, 253–54; idem, 2004, pp. 30–50.

52. Milgrom, 1991, pp. 261–64, 622–25, 1053. On Mil-

grom's interpretation of the "purification offering," see also Gruenwald, 2003, pp. 225–27.

53. Gruenwald, 2003, p. 3.

54. Among various features that constitute his approach, Gilders contrasts symbol with index. A symbol relies on interpretive conventions to define the relationship with its referent. "An *index*, however, is a sign that is connected with its referent as a matter of fact" (Gilders, 2004, p. 8; italics original). He goes on to explain: "While the *meaning* of blood, understood as a symbol, is not apparent simply by observing it, the meaning of blood as an index is immediately evident to the observer who watches for patterns of existential relationship that are marked, indexed, by the handling of the blood" (ibid., p. 81; italics original).

55. Gilders, 2004, pp. 158–80.

56. Heim, 2006, p. 26.

57. Gese, 1981, p. 101.

58. Jones, 1991, p. 9.

59. Jenson, 1995, pp. 25–40.

60. Nicole, 2004, pp. 35–50.

61. Hubert/Mauss, 1899, p. 38: "Il est arbitraire de restreindre ainsi le sens du mot [sacrifice]. Toutes proportions gardées, le mécanisme de la consécration est le même dans tous les cas ; il n'y a donc pas de raison objective pour les distinguer."

62. McClymond, 2008, p. 17. McClymond also states that "there is a fixation on animal sacrifice to such an extent that vegetal and liquid oblations are virtually ignored in theorizing, even though these substances are used far more frequently than animal offerings" (ibid.).

63. Gese, 1981, pp. 105–6.

64. Gese refutes the understanding of the hand-leaning gesture as transferral of sins and immediately concludes that, due to parallels to delegated succession, it must mean identification of the offerer with the sacrificial animal (1981, p. 106). No biblical text, however, explicitly affirms this theory, and the fact that delegated succession occurs only among humans but never between humans and animals makes this theory questionable. However, Gese never ponders the possibility that this gesture could signify declaration of ownership.

65. McClymond, 2008, pp. 33–34, 152–54.

66. George, 2009, p. 161. George, in turn, follows and summarizes the argument of Hurowitz, 1985, pp. 21–30.

67. George, 2009, pp. 184–86 (regarding the Babylonian *Enuma Elish*).

68. These passages are generally attributed to the priestly source (P), one of the four main sources of the Pentateuch. A simpler tent sanctuary looked after by only one person is described in Exodus 33:7-11. It is usually attributed to a different and earlier source, namely that of the Elohist (E).

69. A cubit (Hebrew *'ammâ*) is a frequent linear measure in the Hebrew Bible that was widely used in Near Eastern antiquity (and called "ell" throughout the Middle Ages until early modern times). It corresponds to the distance from the tip of the forefinger to the elbow; as such its absolute length remains relative. However, 1 cubit is generally assumed to equal 0.455 meters or 1.46 feet (17.5 inches), while a margin of error of ±10 percent remains in all efforts to convert this ancient relative standard into a modern absolute one. Further problems to determine its exact equivalence arise from the fact that a "royal cubit" measuring 0.52 meters/1.67 feet likewise existed in the ancient Near East. Yet in 1880 C.E., the Siloam (also called Shiloach) inscription found in Jerusalem states the length of King Hezekiah's water tunnel (mentioned, e.g., in 2 Kings 20:20) as 1,200 cubits (cf. Cogan/Tadmor, 1988, p. 221; the text of the inscription is featured in ibid., p. 337). Its actual length of 546 meters/1,749 feet determines that the standard of measurement here and elsewhere in ancient Israel and Judah was the shorter cubit.

70. On the theme of orientation of sanctuaries in general and the tabernacle in particular, cf. George, 2009, pp. 79–85. George mentions that, contrary to the majority of temples, which faced west, "the spatial practice of orienting temple space on the east-west axis was not something widely shared in Israel throughout its history" (ibid., p. 81).

71. On the opinion that Hebrew *bāmâ* refers less to a geographical but rather to an artificial elevation, see Haran, 1978, pp. 18–25. According to alternative proposals, a *bāmâ* could be a platformlike structure (Vaughan, 1974, pp. 37–54) or designate something different depending on the location and time (Whitney, 1979, p. 147).

72. Cf. Haran, 1978, p. 23.

73. The corrupt cultic practice of Eli's sons consists of their claiming sacrificial meat that came with its fat portions. These, however, were reserved for God (cf. Eberhart, 2002b, pp. 88–96). In addition, it appears that Micah's idol worship (Judg 18:30-31) had continued in Shiloh under the house of Eli (cf. Bodner, 2008, p. 14).

74. Leuchter, 2005, p. 94.

75. Cf. Haran, 1978, p. 43; Sweeney, 2007, pp. 467–70.

76. The temple's dimensions of 60 cubits (88 feet/26.70 meters) in height and 60 cubits in width provided in Ezra 6:3 are usually understood as an exaggeration.

77. See on this opinion for example Elie Assis (with regard to Hag 2:1-9): "Building work having now begun, the ordinariness of the Temple conformed the people's belief that this was not the time to rebuild it. They thought that if God were present He would appear in all His glory, and His house should be glorious likewise" (2008, p. 589; see also Assis, 2007, pp. 514–27).

78. The actual loss of the Ark is mentioned nowhere in the Bible. Therefore, a number of hypotheses, both traditional and scholarly, have been put forward to explain its loss (cf. Day, 2005, pp. 250–70; Kreuzer, 2007, §6). The story that Jeremiah or Josiah hid the Ark, the altar of incense, and the tent of meeting in a cave remains legendary (2 Macc 2:5; for rabbinic references, see Döpp, 1998, p. 111). In contrast, it is conceivable that the Ark was either completely destroyed when Solomon's temple was burned in 586 B.C.E. (De Vaux, 1991, p. 128) or that it was brought to Babylon (*Babylonian Talmud*, tractate *Yoma* 53b; *Jerusalem Talmud*, tractate *Shequalim* 6.1.2), where it disappeared. The enumeration of objects carried away by Nebuchadnezzar's troops, however, does not include the Ark. According to a third explanation, its loss was not due to external assault but to cult reforms or internal religious conflict: either the Ark was removed by Jehoash, or Ahaz (Day, 2005, pp. 255–59); alternatively Manasseh, king of Judah from 687 to 642 B.C.E. "who is pilloried as the greatest of apostates by the Deuteronomistic historian in 2 Kings 21" (Day, 2005, p. 256), placed an Asherah image in the Holy of Holies of Solomon's temple and removed both the Ark and the cherubim (cf. Haran, 1963, pp. 46–58; idem, 1978, pp. 276–88).

79. On the meaning of the Ark as the place of God's presence see below pp. 55–56.

80. It is questionable, however, whether these building projects were motivated through religious sentiments; Herod the Great likewise constructed sanctuaries for pagan deities. The considerable costs of these building campaigns resulted in a heavy tax burden for local Judeans.

81. Josephus writes that the destruction of the Herodian temple was not intended by Titus (*Jewish War* 6:238-66). See also Goodman, 2005, p. 464.

82. Cf. Moffitt, 2006, p. 303.

83. In addition, several reports of minor and major repairs

are found in 1 Kgs 14:27-28; 2 Kgs 12:5-17; 15:35; 16:11-18; 22:3-9.

84. Cogan, 2001, p. 237.

85. The origin and exact meaning of Hebrew dĕbîr is much debated. It could be derived from the Hebrew root dbr ("to speak"), conveying that God speaks from this chamber. This understanding appears to inform the Latin rendering oraculum in the Vulgate. According to different proposals, the term is based on the Arabic term dbr—"to lie behind" and designates "the innermost room" or the chamber "behind" the main chamber (Cogan, 2001, p. 242).

86. These changes to the cult have been described and explained in different ways. Given the progression of the biblical narrative, it indeed makes sense that the older altar of burnt offering utilized in connection with the tabernacle was too small for the number of 142,000 sacrificial animals that were offered for the temple dedication (1 Kgs 8:63; this number itself, however, might be exaggerated; cf. Cogan, 2001, p. 289). According to other proposals, Solomon's father, David, had commissioned a new altar of burnt offering different from that of the tabernacle (Weippert, 1988, pp. 473–74), or Solomon's temple was equipped with an installation similar to a "high place" (Gadegaard, 1978, p. 36). Finally, archaeological finds suggest that large-scale burnt offerings were not yet a regular cultic custom in Israel in the tenth and ninth centuries B.C.E. An altar of burnt offering, at least one of monumental dimensions, would therefore have been missing from Solomon's original temple, but was added later (Zwickel, 1993, pp. 231–32, 246–48). See also Eberhart, 2002a, pp. 322–24.

87. Ehrman, 2004, p. 40. See also Goodman, 2005, p. 460.

88. A detailed description of the Herodian temple is provided in, e.g., Wick, 2002, pp. 52–54.

89. Jacob Milgrom mentions prohibitions in ancient Mesopotamia and Egypt, according to which common people were barred from accessing sanctuaries and watching rituals performed there. In fact, commoners were not even supposed to read, or be familiar with, ritual texts (cf. Milgrom, 1991, pp. 143–44).

90. Cf. Haran, 1978, e.g., pp. 13, 16; Wick, 2002, p. 55; George, 2009, pp. 174–79.

91. In KJV, NKJV, RSV, NRSV, NIV, etc., the Hebrew term mishkān in Exod 40:34 is rendered "tabernacle." This term, however, means primarily "dwelling, residence, domicile."

92. Cf. Haran, 1978, pp. 220–21, 247–59; Day, 2005, pp.

263–64; Kreuzer, 2007, §4. Contrary to the idea that God's presence is linked to the Ark, the book of Deuteronomy describes the Ark rather as a receptacle of the two covenant tables and the book of the law (10:1-5; 31:24-26). However, Ian Wilson has convincingly argued that this function is not dissociate from the divine presence, which is conveyed through the description of the Levitical task in Deut 10:8 (Wilson, 2005, pp. 212–49).

93. Brueggemann, 1997, p. 239.

94. Cf. Assis, 2008, pp. 593–94.

95. Lioy, 2010, p. 36.

96. George, 2009, p. 191.

97. George, 2009, p. 194: "The social nature of that space addressed those new circumstances. Its spatial practices, conceptual space, and symbolic space enabled Israel to create and re-create its social space, and therefore its social identity, wherever it found itself." It may be mentioned that George takes "an agnostic position on the question of the historical existence of the tabernacle" (ibid., p. 12).

98. It should be noted, however, that 11QT does not reference Zerubbabel's temple. On this topic, George J. Brooke concludes: "The *Temple Scroll* thus really refers to two Temples: the first and most fully described is that which should have been built but never was, neither by Solomon nor by the returnees from the exile, neither by Hyrcanus nor by Herod; the second is that which God himself will ultimately create" (2005, p. 425).

99. A more elaborate discussion of how the temple is referenced in the New Testament is presented in Rowland, 2005, pp. 469–83.

100. Cf. Clark, 1959/60, pp. 269–80.

101. Cf. Stemberger, 1995, p. 268.

102. Anderson, 1992, p. 885.

103. Milgrom, 2004, p. 17.

104. The bulk of information in this chapter is based on Eberhart, 2002a, pp. 16–186.

105. Gruenwald, 2003, p. 208.

106. The NRSV translates here and in the following verses "you," while the RSV and NIV render the third person singular masculine of the Hebrew text (and Septuagint) more accurately by translating "he." The NRSV might be interpreted as an attempt to present a gender-inclusive translation. Given the spatial realities of the sanctuary, however, it is unlikely that a female Israelite could present a sacrifice to the priests.

Hannah's sacrifice after weaning her first son Samuel (1 Sam 1:24-25) seems to be exceptional in this regard.

107. Cf. Milgrom, 1991, p. 150; Rendtorff, 2004, p. 33.

108. Cf. Milgrom, 2004, p. 24.

109. Cf. Margueron, 1991, p. 239. Later, however, rabbinic Judaism considered it necessary to explain this gesture (*Babylonian Talmud*, tractate *Hullin* 27a).

110. Cf. Milgrom, 1991, p. 155.

111. Cf. Eberhart, 2006b, §2.1.

112. McClymond, 2008, p. 32.

113. In these passages, the versification between the Hebrew Bible (and Septuagint) differs from that of English Bible versions such as KJV, RSV, NRSV, or NIV.

114. Milgrom, 1991, p. 159.

115. Hebrew *qtr* (*hiph'il*) is sometimes translated as "to turn into smoke" (NRSV; Milgrom, 1991, e.g., pp. 133, 160) or "to offer up in smoke" (NASB), but these equivalents are barely comprehensible for modern English readers. See also the frequent French translation "fair fumer" (e.g., *Traduction Œcuménique de la Bible*).

116. The translation of Hebrew *'iššeh*, especially its connotations to fire, is disputed. Most Bible translations do assume such a connotation and translate *'iššeh* as "offering by fire" (RSV, NRSV) or "offering made by fire" (NKJV, NCV, NIV); see also "offrande consumée par le feu" (*Nouvelle Bible Segond*), "Feueropfer" (*Luther-Übersetzung 1984, Revidierte Elberfelder Bibel*). Recent scholarship, however, has denied such connotations based, for example, on the observation that the Targumim (Aramaic translations of Hebrew Bible texts) render *'iššeh* as *qrbn*-"offering" void of any connotations of fire (cf. Rendtorff, 2004, pp. 63-64; see also Milgrom, 1991, pp. 161-62). Against these arguments, it may be pointed out that Septuagint chooses a variety of equivalents of *'iššeh*, all of which have connotations of fire. For a detailed discussion of these matters, see Eberhart, 2002a, pp. 40-48.

117. Cf. Marx, 2005, p. 139.

118. For a more detailed rationale for this translation, see Eberhart, 2002a, pp. 48-50.

119. This image of YHWH, the living God, is contrasted by that of idols, which cannot smell sacrifices. This is clearly stated in Deut 4:28: "Gods of wood and stone, the work of men's hands, do not see nor hear nor eat nor smell."

120. Cf. Marx, 2005, p. 89.

121. Cf. KJV, NKJV, RSV, NRSV, NIV; see also the frequent French translation "présent" (*Traduction Œcuménique de la Bible, Nouvelle Bible Segond*).

122. Cf. Anderson, 1987, pp. 27–34, 53–54; Milgrom, 1991, p. 196; Marx, 1994, pp. 6–15; Rendtorff, 2004, pp. 87–88.

123. Cf. Ferguson, 1980, p. 1162.

124. Marx, 2005, pp. 81–84. The Hebrew term *qorbānas*, which designates the temple treasury, is derived from *qorbān* (cf. Eberhart, 2010, §3).

125. Marx, 2005, pp. 86–87. It is in this sense that sacrificial rituals represent the internal structure of the cultural and sociopolitical identity of human societies throughout different time periods (cf. Godelier, 1996).

126. Valeri, 1985, p. 66.

127. Cf. Eberhart, 2010, §§1.1; 1.2; 2.

128. Cf. Milgrom, 1991, p. 163.

129. Cf. Anderson, 1987, p. 15; idem, 1992, p. 872; Marx/Grappe, 1998, pp. 26–30; Marx, 2005, pp. 78–81, 88.

130. Cf. Marx, 2005, p. 80: "Il ne s'agit pas de nourrir, mais d'accueillir et d'honorer. Le repas n'est pas une fin en soi. Il est, fondamentalement, un geste d'hospitalité qui permet d'exprimer sa déférence a l'hôte divin."

131. "Grain offering": NKJV, NRSV, NIV; "cereal offering": RSV; Milgrom, 1991, e.g., pp. 177, 179, 196–99. The translation in KJV as "meat offering" demonstrates the degree to which the nature of this type of sacrifice has been misunderstood.

132. Cf. McClymond, 2008, p. 65.

133. Ibid.

134. On the association of olive oil and joy, see Milgrom, 1991, pp. 180, 197.

135. It is interesting to note that according to Vedic cosmology, plants have live essence and are considered to be killed when ritually processed (cf. McClymond, 2008, pp. 47–50).

136. Cf. Yerkes, 1952, p. 24. See also Eberhart, 2005a, p. 44.

137. Cf. RSV; KJV.

138. Cf. ASV.

139. Cf. NLT; see also Vulgate: *hostia pacificorum.*

140. Cf. NRSV; Gilders, 2004, p. 86; McClymond, 2008, p. 57

141. Cf. Milgrom, 1991, pp. 202–25; idem, 2004, pp. 28–29

142. Cf. NIV; New Century Version.

143. Jacob Milgrom explains the difference between "suet" and "fat," the more frequent translation, as follows: "'Suet' refers to the layers of fat beneath the surface of the animal's

skin and around its organs that can be peeled off, in contrast to the fat that is inextricably entwined in the musculature" (2004, p. 29).

144. K. Bodner remarks that this passage might feature "some hierodule humor" (2008, p. 19).

145. Cf. Milgrom, 2000, p. 1623.

146. Milgrom, 2004, p. 30 (the term "sanctum" refers to sacred customs and obligations).

147. Jacob Milgrom proposed the translation "purification offering" (1991, particularly pp. 253–54; see also idem, 2004, e.g., pp. 30–45). The following comments will show that this rendering captures an important aspect of this type of sacrifice, but not its entire effect. Hence the translation "sin offering" is preferable.

148. Cf. Eberhart, 2011d.

149. Cf. Milgrom, 2004, p. 171. For the interpretation of atonement through blood application rites, it is important to note that the most detailed texts on the sin offering in Leviticus 4 and 16 do not presuppose processes of substitutionary identification and incorporation, as Friedhelm Hartenstein stresses (2005, p. 135).

150. Cf. Finlan, 2004, pp. 81–84; Hartenstein, 2005, p. 128. Therefore, modern theorizing on the nature of elimination rituals or sacrifices should avoid treating both as identical as, e.g., in R. Girard's approach (see above, p. 20).

151. This chapter is in part based on Eberhart, 2005a, pp. 48–50.

152. Cf. Blenkinsopp, 2000, p. 450.

153. Anderson, 1992, p. 872 (italics original).

154. See, e.g., the definition of the term *sacrifice* as "an offering accompanied by the ritual killing of the object of the offering" (van Baal, 1976, p. 161).

155. Cf. Anderson, 1992, p. 873.

156. Cf. Yerkes, pp. 6, 24–25.

157. Klingbeil, 2006, p. 26 (italics original); see also Klawans, 2006, e.g., p. 3.

158. This chapter is in part based on Eberhart, 2005a.

159. Cf. Vahrenhorst, 2008, p. 238.

160. Several English Bible versions, however, feature the term "sacrifice" with regard to Jesus in other passages. I will show later that neither the translation of Greek *hilastērion* as "sacrifice of atonement" in Rom 3:25 (NRSV, NIV) nor that of Greek *hilasmos* as "atoning sacrifice" in 1 John 2:2; 4:10 is to be preferred (see below, pp. 114–17).

161. It must be mentioned, however, that not all New Testament passages referring to the blood of Jesus are derived from the sacrificial cult. With the meaning of "shed blood," this term may, as synecdoche, qualify Christ's death as murder (McLean, 1992, p. 546). New Testament example of "blood" with this meaning are found in, e.g., Acts 20:28; Rom 5:9; Eph 1:7; 1 John 5:6, 8; Rev 1:5.

162. This celebration with bread and wine is alternatively known as Eucharist (Mark 14:23), breaking of bread (Acts 2:42, 46; 20:7), (Holy) Communion (from the expression in 1 Cor 10:16), love feast (Jude 12), Last Supper, Lord's Supper, (holy) sacrament of the table, or (Holy) Mass.

163. Most scholars today link the words of institution spoken over the cup with the Mosaic covenant at Mount Sinai; cf. Klauck, 1992, p. 888; Léon-Dufour, 1982, pp. 170–72; Wick, 2002, pp. 248–49; McKnight, 2005, pp. 287–321; Zimmermann, 2005, pp. 89–90; Klawans, 2006, p. 222. Alternative options are Isa 53:12 ("Because he poured out his life unto death and . . . he bore the sin of many"), Jer 31:31 ("I will make a new covenant"), and Zechariah 9:11 ("because of the blood of my covenant with you"), although the latter might already be an early reference to the Mosaic covenant.

164. Cf. Karrer, 2008, p. 216.

165. I need to emphasize that the word "to atone" which translates Greek *hilaskomai*/Hebrew *kipper* is not to be confused with the concept "atonement" that is frequently used as a comprehensive soteriological and theological abstraction.

166. For a reconstruction of this confessional formula, see Kraus, 2008, pp. 195–97.

167. Finlan, 2005, p. 39.

168. See, e.g., NRSV; NIV; further Daly, 1978, pp. 239–40.

169. KJV; NKJV; ASV. See also Vulgate: *propitiationem*.

170. RSV; NAB. See also *Traduction Œcuménique de la Bible* and the rendering *Sühne* ("atonement") in the Luther translation 1984. A convenient survey of the translations of Rom 3:25 in various languages is featured in Ekem, 2007, pp. 80–86.

171. Cf. Breytenbach, 1989, pp. 167–68; Finlan 2005, pp. 40–41 (with reference to scholarship by D. P. Bailey); Ekem, 2007, pp. 80–82; Kraus, 2008, pp. 200–207.

172. NRSV; NIV.

173. Cf. Breytenbach, 1989, pp. 98–99.

174. Cf. Brown, 1982, p. 217.

175. Cf. Watts, 2007, p. 185.

176. Blenkinsopp, 2002, p. 350.

177. Cf. Spieckermann, 2001, p. 136.

178. Cf. Janowski, 1997, pp. 78, 89–90; Groves, 2004, p. 88.

179. Cf. Eberhart, 2002a, pp. 274–78, 286; Schlund, 2005, pp. 400–401.

180. Cf. Eberhart, 2002a, p. 319.

181. Cf. Schlund, 2005, pp. 404–5.

182. Cf. Watts, 2007, p. 183.

183. For a more detailed and in-depth study, see, e.g., Finlan, 2005. The following survey is based in part on Eberhart, 2011b.

184. Cf. Hamerton-Kelly, 1992, pp. 77–79.

185. On this subject, see, in general, Gibson, 2004.

186. Cf. Ehrman, 2004, p. 271; Eberhart, 2005b, pp. 45–46; Jennings, 2009, e.g., pp. 26–45.

187. A comprehensive study of reconciliation is presented by Breytenbach, 1989.